Improve Commu

21 Practices: Develop Conversational Intelligence, Work on Social Skills, Increase Empathy and learn the Art of Persuasion to Achieve Successful Relationships

TABLE OF CONTENTS

Introduction

Communications form the core of human relationships. The way you communicate to people in your family, workplace, and

society at large goes a long way in determining how they perceive you, and in turn how they relate with you. Each one of us needs to make an effort to master the art of conversation.

Some people have strong social skills, naturally. They have no problem starting a conversation with a stranger, joining a group at a social gathering or even speaking in front of an audience. Others, well, they need a little help. You're here reading this book, so chances are, you're in the category that could do with a little boost.

The good news is that social skills can be developed and nurtured. Here we have gone out of our way to give you information on how you can improve your communication abilities. We start off with the basics of holding a conversation. Have you wanted to walk up to a group of people yet hesitated since you were afraid of not finding anything to say? Here we give you some simple conversation starters that are bound to kick-start a conversation.

It is one thing to have a conversation, and it is quite another to have one that lingers in your mind, and that of others, for years to come. What makes a memorable conversation? We delve into the qualities of such a conversation. We keep them simple enough so you can pick them and practice right away.

Communication is not all bliss. Every once in a while you'll encounter skeptics and other annoying people. This book prepares you for such situations. You don't have to get overwhelmed and reciprocate the negativity. You can be the bigger person who navigates the situation and ends up unscathed.

Beyond the social setting, the art of conversation is vital in the workplace as well. Working with a team and coordinating them to achieve a common goal is no mean task. Each member of the team has to learn effective listening. Listening sounds like such an obvious thing, but most of us listen to absent-mindedly while also attending to something else. This book teaches you how to listen effectively so that you can grasp the message in its entirety and also leave the speaker feel valued. Several intricacies of communication at work have been explained here. By communicating effectively at all levels, a business enhances its chances of profitability and growth.

Public speaking has not been left behind. What makes some people so great in front of an audience while others cringe just at the thought of it? You may be surprised to learn that some of those who seem like 'natural' public speakers have taken years of learning, preparation and practice to get there. And so can you. Dig in and find out how to improve your verbal dexterity. We have a challenge as well; simple activities that you can do to improve the various aspects discussed here. Happy reading!

Chapter 1: The Art of conversation

The art of starting and maintaining a conversation is a crucial skill in establishing relationships in all areas of your life. For some, starting a conversation is as easy as breathing. For others, especially introverts, even the thought of it is a source of anxiety. Fortunately, the conversation is a skill that can be learned.

Great conversations almost always start with small talk. Many people avoid small talk at all costs. Sure, it can sound rather pointless to go on and on about the weather or the traffic. But such small talk serves as a precursor for breaking the ice and paving the way for truly significant conversations. Here are some pointers to help you navigate those few (or several) minutes of small talk.

- Be interested in what the other person has to say. Dale Carnegie, the author of the highly acclaimed book How to Win Friends and Influence People, states that showing genuine interest in the people you're speaking to is an essential component for a meaningful conversation. Taking an interest in others makes you interesting. What if you're not interested in the topic at hand? You don't have to be. We learn every day, don't we? Listen and learn. Let your curiosity lead you to ask further questions, to avoid a monologue. Once they have your attention, you can steer the conversation towards a common ground.

- Maintain an active presence with your body language. Avoid fidgeting or looking over your shoulder like you're already mapping your way out. There should also be no scrolling on your phone. This can come across as plain disrespectful. Maintain comfortable eye contact. Such a posture will keep the conversation going.

- What if you initiate small talk and the listener seems blank? Perhaps you're dealing with a conversation rookie who is still getting over social anxiety. Here, you have to speak some more of yourself to prod a response. Let's say you've met in a work seminar and you ask, 'Is this your first time here?' The person answers with a 'no', then awkward silence. You can add something more about yourself. 'Oh, I've been here before, although the speakers are different this year.' The person is then likely to ask about the previous year's speakers. There! You have a conversation going.

Now that you have an idea on how to keep the small talk going, let us delve into the real art of conversation. These tips will guide you into having the sort of conversation that makes the best of yourself, and others.

1. Breaking the ice

A compliment is a great way to start a conversation. Let it be genuine and specific. 'That was a great presentation back there.' 'What an elegant office you have here.' 'That's such a beautiful dog.' A compliment instantly lifts the listener's spirit, and will then look up and pay attention.

Asking for assistance can also be a useful way of initiating dialogue. People appreciate it when they're made to feel useful. Here you're just asking for a little help. You don't want to ask for major help at first meeting; you'll portray yourself as needy. Ask for information. 'Might you happen to know the Wifi password?' 'Do you have yoga classes around here?' 'What do you use on your face? It's glowing.' In the answer is the opportunity to start a discussion.

You can also offer to help. Such offers are not common you know. We're too busy minding our own business. Help someone with luggage. Or to fill a form with a tiny font. Or to find their way in a conference venue. These people will speak to you, out of gratitude if nothing else.

Once you've broken the ice, you can delve into the conversation and see where it takes you.

2. Deepen the conversation

Small talk is only good for the onset, but it's hardly fulfilling. There's isn't so much you can say about the weather or how your day is going. Eventually, people will get bored and trail off. You have to make a deliberate effort to add depth to the conversation. 'What line of work are you in?' Such a question at a work conference will get people talking about their jobs. If you bump into a neighbor picking kids from school, you can inquire about what they like about that particular school. That is likely to lead to a conversation about schools and education as a whole. A deep conversation keeps people interested and ultimately leads to stronger relationships.

3. Get a common ground

Sometimes you will hold a conversation with strangers from different worlds in terms of residency, careers, views, and general likes. What can you talk about? Look for common ground. No matter how diverse you are, you can always find common ground. To begin with, you're already in the same location. That's already common ground. Are you attending the same meeting? Or living in the same neighborhood? Or traveling on the same flight? When you bring up what you have in common, you strike an instant connection. From there you can create a meaningful conversation.

4. Maintain a positive attitude

Nobody wants to listen to a whiner, especially one you just met. If you're always complaining, people will avoid you. Make a better initial impression. Say something nice. Compliment the event, the speakers or the organizers. Positivity draws attention and makes people want to listen to you. If you have grievances about the boss, food, flight, services and whatever else could be getting on your nerves, channel those grievances to the right people. Don't rant about them to people who can't change them. At best, they'll whine with you'll and achieve nothing. At worst, they'll look for the nearest exit to get away from you.

5. Balance speaking and listening

Don't be so enthusiastic about making conversation that you keep talking and talking. Coach and psychiatrist Dr. Mark Goulston, the author of the communication handbook Just Listen, suggests that you should not speak for more than 20 seconds at a time. Give your listener time to contribute. Otherwise, you'll come across as self-absorbed. If you happen to be engaging someone who seems to be doing all the talking, make an effort to contribute.

6. Learn to handle divergent views

Listening to people does not necessarily mean that you agree with what they're saying. It means that you respect their opinions. As a rule, steer away from controversial topics when talking to new people. Should they come up anyway, express your thoughts rationally and give an opportunity to the other person to do the same. Under any circumstances, the conversations should not degenerate to verbal wars.

Practice these tips and watch your conversation skills get better. Also make an effort to keep informed on current issues, as well as developments in your field of work. The art of conversation is incomplete without corresponding content. Getting people to listen to you is not always easy, so when they finally do, give them their time's worth.

Chapter 2: Common Communication Barriers

It is one thing to talk, and quite another to be heard and understood. In most cases, we miss out on the message being communicated simply because we're not listening. We're so accustomed to multi-tasking that we hardly ever attend to just one activity at a time. Listening is no exception. We often lack attention, interest, are distracted or consider the information irrelevant. This forms the first barrier to communication. Somebody is talking, but the listener is not absorbing the information. Other barriers include:

1. Information overload

This happens where there is so much information, and the brain cannot process it all. Think of the many hours you spend online every day. What exactly are you reading or watching? Can you summarize the information you've come across after an hour online? Probably not. You were clicking one website after the other, watching videos, checking out your friends' profiles on social media and so on. No sooner have you started paying attention to one thing, than you spot a link for something that looks more interesting. You have so much information competing for your attention, you end up absorbing none of it. What a waste of time!

You can prevent this by deciding exactly what it is you need to do online. If you're going to research for a project, stick to that and give yourself a timeline. If you're constantly getting distracted by social media sites such as Facebook and Instagram, you can block them temporarily. If you don't know how to go about blocking them, you're even luckier. Have someone block them for you. You don't know how to unblock them either; right? Good! Now you'll have to do without them. Concentrate on the important matters - actually productive information.

2. Language barriers

You may have encountered this at an international conference. While you may have interpreters for the formal part of the event, informal interactions can get tricky. You find yourself at your lunch table with people from other organizations that you can actually learn something from, yet you can hardly exchange a sentence. Even when some effort has been made to learn the language, accents may still come in the way. You also encounter language barriers when you're an international student, or when visiting another country or continent. If the engagement is only short-term, you can somehow survive. If it's long-term, then learn the language. There are plenty of translation apps, but they mostly work for written content. You may come across a few dealing with the spoken word. You can use them for some time as you hone your new language.

3. Slang and Other Jargon

The use of slang is common in some neighborhoods. Slang is an informal language that is coined randomly, and grow to become accepted language. For instance, missing a class or meeting may be referred to as 'skiving.' The TV is known as 'telly.' 'Cuppa' is used to refer to a cupful – A 'cuppa' coffee. Some of these are distortions of the real words, while others are just made up. One day someone throws in a catchy queer phrase into a song, next thing you know people have incorporated it into their language.

You may be aware of some of these slang words. To you, they're as correct as any other. To somebody else, they may be incorrect or even strange. Some people will not entertain slang in official communication. Others do not mind. Get to know whom you're dealing with, so that you can communicate in a manner that is deemed fit.

4. Emotional barriers

We often make assumptions about who will listen to us and who will not. Someone going through a rough time fails to communicate believing nobody will care. This must be the reason we have so many people with dark issues which they've bottled inside for years. This may be cases of abuse, rejection, assault, violence, and so on. Communication is hindered by fear of victimization.

Should you happen to be in this category, you do not have to suffer in silence. Keeping things inside will only aggravate the harm. You can talk to someone around you, to your family, friend or colleague. You may be surprised that other people have gone through similar circumstances. If you'd rather talk to a stranger for privacy purposes, there are certified counselors available. Their code of ethics provides for non-disclosure. They say a problem shared is half solved. Just by speaking out, you have made the first step towards healing.

5. Perception differences

One person may perceive an issue different from the other. This is common between men and women. For instance, what may seem like love to a man may not be so with the woman.

Sex represents love to a woman, not so to a man. The woman might even assume they're in a relationship and get deeply attached, even making their future plans in her mind. To the man, well, they're just having a good time.

In the workplace, when the boss sends you a memo for the late submission of reports, what does that mean? The boss does not like me? That you'll receive a poor valuation? That you're about to be fired? It could be just what it is; a warning so you can submit on time if the future. The rest could be just your perceptions.

Instead of assuming, you can just speak it out. Ask for clarification. You might act on assumptions only to find out that you were all wrong.

6. Hearing impairments

Every once in a while, you will encounter somebody who is partially and totally deaf. Do you know any sign language? It does not hurt to know the basics. People with disabilities need to be accommodated too. Should you have some in the workplace, the entire team should make an effort to communicate with them. They want to be productive just like anyone else.

Your parents could have partial deafness as they age. You find that you have to shout for them to hear. You can try hearing aid; they're simple external devices that work for most people. Be patient with those with hearing disabilities, remember in a twist of fate, that could be you.

Successful communication involves talking, hearing and understanding. If any of these steps are compromised, then significant communication has not taken place. In addition to working towards improving conversational skills, we should also eliminate the barriers along the way.

Chapter 3: Improve Your Personality for Quality Conversation

What do people mean when they say that you have a good personality? Mostly they mean that you're warm, likable, and a pleasure to be around. Personality is basically the thinking and behavior pattern that makes one unique.

Just as we alter or improve our physical appearance to get to a certain standard that we deem attractive, so can we improve our personality. In fact, we should put more emphasis on personality as opposed to physical traits. As far as opportunities are concerned, looks will get you through the door, but it is the personality to keep you there. Research done among fortune 500 CEOs shows that their main consideration when hiring, after the experience, is personality.

Your personality determines your ability to communicate with those around you and eventually form lasting relationships. Here's how you can improve your personality.

1. Better listening

Listening sounds like such an obvious activity that we all do even without a second thought. However, most of us are doing it wrong. We only half listen as we attend to other matters or browse on our phones. Effective listening involves paying full attention to the speaker. Look up. Turn the body towards the speaker. Maintain eye contact. Nod along the way. Restate and ask questions where necessary. It is not enough to be listening; it is just as important for the listener to know that you're listening.

In a world so accustomed to multitasking, you stand out when you listen attentively. People will gravitate towards you since your listening makes them feel valued and appreciated. They will be encouraged to open up, knowing that you're taking in every detail. Such are the conversations that make an impact.

2. Stay informed

It is one thing to have the ability to say something, and it's quite another to have something valuable to say. Maybe the ability to communicate comes easily to you. You're confident enough to speak in various spheres. However, do you have the content to match? People get bored with shallow talk really fast. They will be drawn by your speaking ability but will lose interest as so as they learn that you have nothing meaningful to say.

We're in the age of information, with so much of it at the palm of our hands. Yet even then, you have to make a conscious decision to go for the right information. Instead of spending hours online browsing through the profiles of friends, foes, and celebrities, endeavor to teach yourself something meaningful. Keep abreast of current affairs. Dig out the new trends in your industry. Study what is happening in politics, business, sports, entertainment and any other field of interest.

No matter what direction the conversation takes, you'll have something to say. You'll have an opinion. Your arguments will be informative and intellectually stimulating. People will listen to you and learn something new.

3. Positive attitude

Nobody wants to listen to a whiner. Even if things are actually bad, we don't want to keep being reminded. If you're not happy with the boss, or your mother-in-law, or the traffic, or the status of your bank account, you don't have to moan about them all day long. Most people will utilize the first chance to get away from you, while those who will stay and listen will not help you at all. If you actually have grievances like we all do, direct them to the relevant entities who can do something about them.

Look for something positive to say in conversation. Compliment. Appreciate. Encourage. Give hope. Point out the positives even in a difficult situation. With so much negativity around us, your positive attitude will be a welcome break, and everybody who meets you will be glad they did.

4. Grooming

Your dressing and body physique makes the first impression. People will have an opinion of you even before you get a word out of your mouth. Grooming comes easy for some. They have an eye for style. They can put together a splendid outfit without much effort. Then we have, well, the rest. They throw on the first thing they find in the morning. Or whatever they haven't worn in a while. Or the only clean clothes they got. These are people who have had the same haircut for years. And don't know the price of a manicure.

Please note that poor grooming does not mean that you're a terrible person. You could be an excellent performer at work, a productive member of society and doting to your family. Those who know you might overlook your grooming, but remember they're only a small group. The rest of us judge the book by the cover.

Declutter your closet and throw out those flabby clothes. Get shopping. If shopping is not your thing, you can enlist the help of a stylist. Stylists can take your measurements and shop even in your absence. Get a new haircut. Perhaps some color in your hair would also look good, too. A manicure and pedicure could come in handy too. Get moving if you're out of shape. Once your first impression speaks highly of you, you attract the right attention that leads to productive conversations.

5. Outgoing

Go out and meet new people. Know their cultures, languages, beliefs, habits, and so on. If you had any prejudices against people of a different background, you may be surprised how misleading they could be. Our society is fond of labeling. Black men are criminals. Mexicans are illegal migrants. Muslims are terrorists. You hear these statements over and over again until they begin to sound true. If you don't step out of your familiar territory and meet these people, you will find yourself labeling them as well.

Meeting and interacting with people of different backgrounds teaches you that we're all just human. Those Muslims that you're labeling are trying to get by just like you. They're thinking of careers, bills, and educating their children, just like the rest of us.

An outgoing personality will make you more empathetic and tolerant. You will then be in a position to converse comfortably with people from diverse backgrounds.

6. Confidence

We saved the best for last. Confidence is a trait that will get you through many doors. A confident person is regarded as competent and skilled. Some people are naturally confident, others not quite. If you fall into the second category, you will be glad to know that confidence can actually be nurtured. Walk with your head high. Shake hands firmly. Project your voice with clarity when you speak. Master your content so you're saying the right thing. Hone your public speaking skills. Confidence attracts people to you, and the conversations you have lead to great relationships.

Chapter 4: Verbal Dexterity

If you Google the most famous speeches in history, you will come across the likes of Martin Luther King, Barrack Obama, Nelson Mandela, Malcolm X, among others. One term can be used to describe the speaking prowess of these world leaders - verbal dexterity. They have mastered the art of delivering speeches. Thousands gather to hear them speak. Their speeches have received millions of views on Youtube, and the numbers continue to grow. You can tell some repeat viewers. They keep watching and listening to them over and over again, stoked by their confidence and eloquence.

Are these speakers different from the rest of us? Were they born pros or did they hone their skills along the way? Well, most of it comes from learning and practice. Some even have teams that help them prepare for weeks or even months before delivering the speech. That's consoling. If they can sharpen their listening skills, so can you. You may not rise to the world stage like they did (and then again, you just might), but you can also speak with conviction in your circle of influence.

1.Content

The content of these speeches was informed by the activities that these leaders had been involved in for years. Martin Luther King spoke passionately about the civil rights movements and the oppression of the black. These were matters that he has been involved in for years. He knew them by heart. He simply spoke his heart out.

If you aspire to speak as they did, stick to the content that is in your line of work. If you're a teacher, for instance, you'll be better placed to speak about the reforms required in the education center. If you're a nurse, you can draw the attention of the people towards the challenges faced by the health practitioners and patients in the face of unstable health insurance. Go on, find your niche. Mastering that content is a first step in enhancing your verbal dexterity.

2.Passion

It is one thing to know what is happening in your country or community, and it is quite another to care. These leaders that we speak about here cared deeply for the people in their oppression. Mandela stood up against apartheid oppression. He stated on several occasions that he was prepared to die for that cause.

Do you have something that you're passionate about? Do you feel the need to stand up for it? Can you do so consistently? It does not have to be confrontational. It just has to be close to your heart. Passion also leads you to get more information. If you're passionate about the need to rid the world of plastic pollution, for instance, you will read through any relevant information. You will be aware of the highest polluting companies, the measures the government is putting in place, any relevant bills, organizations working towards tackling the problem and so on. When you speak on the topic, your speech will be heartfelt, passionate and enlightening.

Once you have these two, the rest is presentation skills that you can learn. Public speaking skills such as stage presence, tonal variation, body language, and technology have been covered in a different chapter in detail. The bottom line is to have the basics in place, then learn and practice the rest.

As exemplified by these leaders, verbal dexterity can change the world. Speaking with passion and conviction gets people to listen to you and heed to your call. Sharpen your verbal dexterity today; the world is waiting to hear your voice.

Chapter 5: Empathic Listening

Empathic listening involves feeling the emotions behind the words spoken. This is achieved by imagining yourself in the situation of the speaker in order to understand the feelings that lead to various decisions and actions. Why would you want to listen to someone like this? Because you care. What they have to say is important to you, as is their welfare. From home, the workplace and the community, emphatic listening will endear you to everyone you come across. It sounds like a good idea, right? Here's how to be an empathic listener:

1. Attentive listening

Dedicate your full attention to listening, without doing anything else on the side. Stop scrolling on your phone or computer. Stop typing. Stop playing music on the background. Stop eating. Turn your body to face the speaker and maintain eye contact. Nod as necessary. Observe the facial expressions, gestures, and general body language.

It is not enough to listen; it is just as important to let the speaker know that you're listening. This assurance makes it easier to open up. Have you had one of those conversations where the listener turns attention to something else midway, such as replying to a message? You then pose to give him/her time to finish the task. But alas; they tell you to proceed. 'Go on, I'm still listening.' In most cases, this will be someone senior to you, so you will have no choice but to oblige. You attempt to carry on with the conversation, but you're deflated. You don't speak as well as before. It turns out the quality of listening affects the quality of speaking.

In this regard, attentive listening encourages the speaker to fully open up. This is what separates counselors from the rest of us. No wonder they manage to get people to open up on issues they've kept inside for years.

Attentive listening in the workplace encourages productive communication. Workers know that they can go to their bosses and express exactly how they feel. Customers can also give their honest feedback.

2. Non-judgmental listening

Following the point on attentive listening, try to listen without forming an opinion on what is being said. Listen to understand, not to answer. If you let your mind wander, you'll begin to mentally critique what you're listening to. This changes your perception and affects your listening.

It is natural to lean towards judgment. We often do it subconsciously. You have already set standards in your mind regarding how people should behave when faced with various situations. Everything is in black and white; right or wrong. While you're listening, you're also trying to classify the decisions and actions in the story as either right or wrong. How much can be achieved with such an attitude? Not much. You will even miss out on some bits of information as you're busy adjudicating.

Be cognizant of your thoughts, so you can catch them whenever they turn away from the conversation. Instead of labeling actions as right or wrong, seek to know the circumstances leading there. Ask follow-up questions. The answers will help you identify with the speaker and understand why they chose to act the way they did. While at it, don't interrupt. It can be hard to get back to a line of thought once interrupted.

3. Rephrase

We often judge because we feel the need to say something in the conversation. We end up saying something like, 'how could you take him back after all he had done to you?' which is just plain judgmental. Instead, you can rephrase what has already been said. Repeat what you have understood from the conversation in different words. 'So he convinced you that he had gone for counseling and was now a changed man?'

Rephrasing keeps your thoughts from straying. You remain attentive so that should you have to reword something, you should get it right. Restating assures the listener that you're attentive, and encourages the conversation to keep going.

4. Moments of silence

Silence in a conversation does not have to be awkward. In empathic listening, moments of silence are not only allowed, but also encouraged. Opening up about sensitive matters takes a lot of energy. The speaker may have broken down and cried at some point. The listener also needs time to absorb what has been said. In moments of silence, both catch their breath.

Observe the speaker during the silence. If a hand of comfort is needed, you can offer a pat on the back or a rub on the back of the hand. Ask a follow-up question when ready to continue.

Silence does not make you a bad listener. Resist the temptation to barge in and 'salvage' the moment. Silence is actually a healthy part of communication.

5. End on a positive note

No matter how difficult the conversation was, it should end on a positive note. Find something good that can come out of the situation. If you're speaking to a lady who has just come out of an abusive relationship like in the conversation above, point out something constructive about the episode. For instance, she can now tell the signs of an abusive partner from the onset. She can share such information with others to help them avoid such relationships. She can also help those in abusive relationships or those who had just quit. In short, the experience equips her with the knowledge that she can use to impact society.

6. Follow-up

The conversation should not end when the two of you part ways. The talk should be the beginning. It is true that a problem shared is a problem half-solved. What about the other half? It comes in what is done after the problem is shared. Here, we're referring to a case of counseling where someone comes to you with a problem. You might have made some recommendations on how to move forward. Were they implemented? Was there any noticeable change? Does the burden feel any lighter? Monitor the situation so you can know how to proceed from there.

Benefits of Empathic Listening

How do you feel when someone listens to you attentively, patiently and without judgment? You feel valued and appreciated. In a world that is so quick to judge, knowing that you'll not be judged will encourage you to speak your mind and heart.

Listening in this way also strengthens relationships. True bonds are formed between people who can talk about anything. It is a lonely world. Even with hours spent on social media talking to friends and strangers, many people do not have someone they can open up to about the issues going on in their lives. Setting yourself apart as an empathic listener will draw people to you, and you'll be a treasure to those you interact with.

Finally, empathic listening ensures that communication actually takes place, because someone is actually listening. Very often we have someone who is talking, but the would-be listener is either distracted or disinterested. The communication chain is broken midway. Follow the tips above to become an empathic listener, and watch the relationships with people around you shift for the better.

Chapter 6: Improve your Relationships for Better Communication

The ability to communicate effectively with your partner is one that you build over time. The strength of your bond determines the quality of your communication. This, in turn, determines its longevity.

Relationships have never been as fickle as they are today. Separation and divorce cases have become so common, it is no longer news. It is not unusual to see a couple in its 20s already divorced. What is it that we're doing wrong? We have several older couples that have been together for decades, and back then it was the norm.

We need to put in conscious effort into our relationships. Healthy relationships translate into a healthy society. We definitely need to do better.

1. Love yourself

This already sounds like a cliché statement, right? You must have heard it so many times before. Either way, it does not lose its validity. A relationship is not a combination of 2 halves. It is the bringing together of 2 whole people to complement each other. Your partner is not there to complete you. You're already whole. Or at least you should be.

Create a life for yourself. Have a job, business, hobby, friends or any other thing that fascinates you. Attend to your interests. Treat your body and mind. Many relationships are failing because people are over-relying on their partners. It is not the duty of your partner to make you happy. If you have not managed to find happiness in all those years, don't you think it's a huge task to place on someone else? Create the life that you want, then invite your partner to share in the joy.

2. Be honest

Lies destroy a lot of relationships. Can you be trusted by your partner? Can he or she trust you to do exactly as you agreed? Can you remain faithful in your relationship? What is the worst that your partner can do if you actually told the truth?

They say that lies have a very short life span. Here's another one: there are 3 things that you cannot hide; the sun, the moon, and the truth. Sooner or later, the truth comes out. The liar may try to tell another lie to cover up for the first one. Why go through so much trouble?

Lies then breed mistrust. You begin to doubt every word that comes out of your partner's mouth. When trust is broken, things are never the same. They say that broken trust is like a broken vase. You can glue it back together, but it will never be the same again.

Cultivate a culture of honesty where you tell things as they are, even when they're bad. Avoid overreacting in anger when you're told the truth. Take time to calm down then you can talk it over. Such an approach will encourage your partner to tell the truth.

3. Connect

We're often preoccupied with the developments of our lives that we forget to make time for our significant other. Granted, those bills will not pay themselves. But there has to be a limit. You may be out there hell-bent on chasing the dollar to give your family a better life, but by the time you get your money together, you have no family to speak of.

Make it a priority to bond with your partner. Set aside time and observe it as strictly as you observe your work schedule. Spend quality time without your phones or any other distractions. Get to know how each other is doing beyond the surface. You may be assuming that your partner is fine just because he/she is going on with life as normal, but that could be far from it. Discuss deeper matters; mental health, job satisfaction, inner battles, goals, dreams and so on.

Go for the holidays. Go for dates. Visit places that are significant to your relationship. Go clubbing and dancing, just as you did when you were younger. That will add a breath of fresh air to your relationship.

4. Empathy

In the world acclaimed relationship book *Men are from Mars; Women from Venus*, the author John gray expounds that men and women have very different needs. They view the world differently. Men have a hard time understanding why a woman would be so bothered by some dress at the store not fitting. They will even argue with the attendant when told to try one a size bigger. Matters of weight are close to their hearts. They often ask all legendary 'do I look fat in these?' Can you empathize with your wife in that situation? Similarly, women hardly understand why men mourn when a team loses. You'd think somebody died!

Here both parties will have their empathy tested. Empathy involves stepping into the shoes of your partner so you can feel their emotions, and see things from their point of view. In this case, the husband can suggest that the wife joins a fitness club so that the dress will eventually fit. The wife can, in turn, sympathize with the guy on his loss, and perhaps cook him his favorite meal to make him feel better. It sounds like a good idea, right?

5. Productive conflict

Disagreements can make or break your relationship. In most cases, they break. But you can handle them such that they even leave your bond stronger. Agree to set aside some conflict time and place. Even if you're dealing with an issue, don't result in a shouting match all over the house. Sometimes the verbal wall even goes beyond your house. Set aside a time when you're both relaxed. Let's say a Saturday afternoon. Set the place as well. Perhaps in the study room or in the backyard, since the outdoors makes everything better. There you can outline all your issues, discuss them and find the way forward. This does not mean that you will always agree. But you can agree to disagree. You can choose to respect each other's opinions even when you don't agree with it.

6. Spend time alone

The quality of your relationship is determined by the status of the 2 of you. If either of you is fatigued, stressed, disgruntled, dissatisfied or depressed, it will end up affecting both of you. It is a good idea to take time alone to refresh. Go do the things that make you happy. Go shop for new clothes. Get a haircut, a massage or a spa treatment. You can even take a brief holiday. Take this moment to rejuvenate, heal and reflect. By the time you go back to your partner, you will be a refreshed person, and it will mirror your relationship.

These tips should help you strengthen your relationship, so you can go through the ups and downs of life together. With such a bond, your communication will be so much better.

Chapter 7: Make your Conversations Unique and Memorable

We hold so many conversations in our daily lives with family, colleagues, business associates, acquaintances, bosses, neighbors, and even strangers. Most of them are soon forgotten; then there are those that linger in our minds for a long time. What separates the common conversation from truly great ones? Here's how to have unique conversations:

1. Full concentration

We often hold conversations when also concentrating on something else; a task, TV or phone. Multitasking has become a standard operating procedure. By the end of the conversation, neither party can outline what was said in the conversation. Make your conversation unique by paying full attention. Maintain a steady 70 – 80% eye contact. It will be a refreshing change for people that are used to being listened to just partially. If you're a fan of meditation, we call this listening mindfully. Mindfulness basically refers to living at the moment and enjoying all aspects of it. When you listen mindfully, you're attentive to every detail. The speaker will feel valued, appreciated and cared for, and will have no problem opening up.

2. Compliments

Throw in a genuine kind word here and there. This comes in handy at the beginning of a conversation. It helps break the ice and places the discussion on a positive stand. As the conversations go on, you can identify more areas that deserve a compliment. Let's say people are talking about their careers. Somebody in the group mentions that they work for a particular real estate company. You happen to know that (remember what we said about staying informed?) that the company is undertaking a massive project in the neighboring county. You can congratulate the speaker on the work 'they' are doing. Let the compliments be brief; just a sentence or two. The effect is still outstanding. The receiver feels noticed, appreciated and validated. With such a lifted spirit, the conversation is bound to be remembered for a long time.

3. Balance speaking and listening

This is a balance that is so often lacking, yet even those responsible for it could be doing so subconsciously. There are those self-absorbed people that will go on a monologue while everybody else is quiet. Such a scenario may even be thought of as a positive thing; 'they're all letting me speak since I'm the expert.' Unless you're giving a speech to an audience, dominating the dialogue as such is inappropriate. You risk coming across as proud and arrogant. However well you know the subject matter, or how good your oratory skills are, give the others an opportunity to speak. Show genuine interest in what they have to say. If you're in a group, let everyone say something.

You may be on the other side of the coin, where you hardly say anything in conversations. You're a quiet listener. Anything wrong with this approach? Absolutely. A conversation is a team effort. Whether you're engaging one other person or a group of people, all parties should participate. When you remain silent, the interlocutor(s) are inwardly trying to figure out why. Is the conversation boring? Are you not interested in the topic of discussion? Or are you devoid of content to contribute? See? You're taking their mental energy away from the conversation and tasking them with the burden of trying to interpret your actions. All this can be avoided if you contribute periodically, and facilitate a truly memorable conversation.

4. Steer the conversation

Once you break the ice with small talk, don't dwell there for long. Small-talk is unfulfilling and gets people easily bored. Pick cues of the interlocutor's interests from the conversation. From there, direct the conversation towards a deeper issue. From casual comments about the speakers in a conference, you can ask a question like, 'what do you expect the presenters will address this afternoon?' You can then talk about your expectations for the meeting and other relevant matters concerning the event.

Similarly, a random comment about sleeping in for the weekend can be turned into a more meaningful conversation about rest, unwinding, working hard vs working smart, work-related stress and so on. A deep conversation makes a lasting impression.

5. Use technology

We have stated before that you should avoid your gadgets when having a conversation, but isn't there an exception to every rule? If you've tried all means and the conversation still ends up stalling, you can compromise a bit. Refer to something interesting, informative, funny or relevant that you can come across online. Say something like; 'have you watched this documentary on the long-term effects of these Chinese loans?' Go ahead and steam the clip from your phone or laptop. It does not have to belong. And if it is, you don't have to watch the whole of it.

As the people turn their attention to the video, you will have time to catch a breath. Trying to keep a conversation going can be draining, you know. The conversation will then resume on a new angle. People will now be giving their views on what they just watched. Others could take the queue and also share the content they have on their gadgets. You all can then have something in common to speak about.

6. Exit politely

Sometimes, even after your best effort, the conversation cannot seem to gain traction. You do not have to suffer endlessly. You can excuse yourself. Begin by summarizing what you guys last spoke about. For instance, in the video above, you can say something like, 'that is a whole lot of money to expect a third-world country to pay back in such a short time.' Then ask to leave. Thank them for their time and state that you need to leave to attend to a different matter and walk out gracefully.

Did you know that we have an App that helps you get out of awkward situations by calling you? You heard that right. You press some buttons on the App then put it back into your bag or pocket. After a couple of minutes, your phone rings. Mr. App calling; thank you very much. You excuse yourself to take the call, then you can plan your exit from there. This definitely does not sound like the most ethical thing to do. But let's face it, there are those situations that are so bad, they call for something this radical. Otherwise, in normal uncomfortable situations, you should be in a position to excuse yourself and leave politely.

Such unique conversations make people want to talk to your time and again. You'll be the magnet in the room; people will gravitate towards you. Influencing people will come easy for you. In the process, you'll form lasting relationships that will positively affect your life.

Chapter 8: Body Language Guide

There is more to communication than just speaking. Your movements, postures, and gestures, whether conscious or not, play a major role in the perception of the message by the listener. You could be saying one thing, yet your body is communicating something different. You don't want such a contract, especially when you're speaking in front of an audience. You also read the body language of those you're speaking to so that you can adjust the conversation accordingly. Here are various instances where body language can be employed:

Listening: Turn your head and body towards your interlocutor. Avoid fidgeting with your phone or computer. No multi-tasking. Nod periodically as necessary. What if you don't do these things but listen anyway; you may ask. Well, the issue here is not just about listening. You have to appear to be listening as well. The speaker should be aware that you're listening attentively. Such listening leaves the person feeling valued, appreciated and deemed worthy of undivided attention.

Shaking Hands: Give firm handshakes and linger for a moment. This signifies confidence. Handshakes are the symbol of solidity and unity the world over. Political leaders shake hands when forming a coalition. Business leaders shake hands when signing contracts. In boardrooms the world over, hands are shaken to signify agreements. Such is the power of a handshake. A research conducted by the Income Center for Trade shows that shaking hands doubles the chances of remembering a person. People become friendlier after shaking hands, as a bond has already been created.

Smiling: The power of a smile cannot be over-emphasized. It is said that it is the most effective curve and also the best make-up that you can wear on your face. A smile disarms you and portrays you as approachable and cooperative. People will find it easier to strike a conversation with you. Should you be the one to start the conversation, then people will be more receptive to you. A smile makes you more attractive. And people around you smile right back at you. That lifts your spirits. The smile isn't just for others; it's for you too.

Agreement: Here's one that is not very common. In the boardroom, people tend to mirror the body language of people that they agree with. For instance, if you make a point that is approved, and you happen to be sitting up with a hand on your chin, the other participants with subconsciously place their hands on their chins. It's like their way of saying that they can see what you see. The next time you're making a presentation, this is an interesting one that you can look out for. If nobody is replicating your body language, you may be alone in the ideas you're presenting.

Calm voice: A rational tone says that you're in control. You're not letting the things around you get into your head. Speak calmly even when your emotions tell you otherwise. Shouting will portray you as downright rude and arrogant. On the other hand, whispering labels you as timid. When you feel overwhelmed, take a few moments to breathe deeply before you start talking.

Power pose: Here's how to pose like a boss. Ok, at least an aspiring boss. Lean back on the office chair with hands behind your head, and legs on the desk. Familiar pose? Yes, probably from a movie, portraying the boss. This pose actually releases hormones that reduce stress. A similar effect can be achieved by standing with legs and arms stretched wide.

Effective body language ensures that you're portraying the right message. Remember it also makes the first impression, even before you speak a word. Take that opportunity to make a good impression and ensure that you're perceived positively.

We also have negative body language which we sometimes express subconsciously. Consider a situation such as a job interview. Interviewers are interested in what you say as well as what you don't say. They're watching you keenly trying to pick clues of your personality and character. Here are some instances where your body language gives a negative impression.

Slouching: Sitting or walking around with drooping shoulders is seen to be a sign of disinterest or low self-esteem. It will be assumed that you're not really interested in the job (maybe you just have bills to pay) or you have a poor self-image.

Fidgeting: If you can't sit still without fiddling your arms or legs, you end up looking anxious. It is assumed that you're poor in handling pressure, and you lack confidence.

Folded arms: Signifies an aggressive, defensive or closed person who others will have a hard time approaching. It is even suggested that in a meeting, people who sit with their arms closed retain less information. But then again, you can argue that it is simply because they're not writing.

Rapid nodding: You seem to be agreeing with everything that is being said, but is that a positive trait? Are you genuinely convinced or are you trying to appear so in an effort to impress the panel? That kind of nodding portrays you as one without an opinion and one who is quick to please.

Very close proximity: Do you move too close when you're speaking to people? That portrays you as one who does not respect boundaries. In addition, you just make people uncomfortable.

How's this for a first impression? Definitely not good. You'll be lucky to be considered for the job. Yet most of these are just assumptions. You could be folding your arms yet you're as friendly as they come, and you're also paying attention. But the panel is seeing something different. Since it's their opinion that counts here, you may as well be cautious. Practice the correct body language even when you're not under scrutiny, and when the time comes when somebody is observing you such as in this scenario, you'll come out clean.

Chapter 9: Communicating with Difficult People

Difficult people thrive in defying logic; or do they have a different kind of logic? It's hard to tell. While some of them are oblivious to the negative impact of their attitude, others are fully aware of the distress they cause, and it does not bother them much.

Whenever you encounter an unreasonable person, the first instinct tells you to reciprocate the exact same attitude. And why not? They started it anyway, right? This is common in a business where disgruntled customers want to give everyone a piece of their mind. Sometimes they have a legitimate concern. Sometimes not. In fact, they could be on the wrong. Perhaps you should show them that you can yell too, right?

This sounds like an easy approach. However, if you're here reading this book on communication skills, you must be interested in improving your conversation intelligence. You're keen on developing your social skills, improving empathy, learning the art of persuasion and achieving successful relationships all around. Therefore, when you encounter difficult people, you must choose to be the bigger person and deal with the situation rationally.

1. What's the need?

What is the interlocutor asking for? Listen. Separate the person from the issue. Behind the altercation, there is a real need to be addressed. If a customer is being difficult, perhaps he's been offered poor service or maybe poor quality items. What can you offer? Perhaps you can replace the particular items? Or offer a better service. Perhaps you can even throw in a free item as an apology. On the other hand, you will find that the customer is on the wrong. Maybe he's demanding for a warranty when the set period has already lapsed. Or when the damage was caused by poor handling. Here you can only try and explain calmly.

2. Don't make demands

Once a person begins being unruly, it is tempting to also shout him into submission by ordering him to keep quiet, sit down, calm down, leave and so on. But remember you're dealing with a person who is already agitated. Additional orders will only make matters worse.

3. Involve others

If you're certain that you're in the right, involve other people. If you're at work, call your coworkers. If not, you can involve your family, friends, and even strangers. Maybe somebody else will bring a different approach and the person will listen. If there are more people on your side, even if the person does not agree with you, he's likely to back down.

4. No laughing/smiling

This is not one of those situations where a smile or laughter makes things better. Difficult people do not exactly function like the rest of us do. Trying to appear pleasant will only agitate them further. Maintain a calm and composed face that only signifies that you're doing what you can to remedy the situation.

5. Remain calm

This one is definitely easier said than done. When anger is directed to you, it very quickly stirs anger in you. The problem here is not feeling angry, but letting the anger control your actions. You can control your anger (we have covered that extensively in another topic) and remain calm. Surprise the aggressor who expects you to be equally angry. He'll realize that he's the only angry one. Now that sort of embarrassing; right? He's likely to calm down on his own volition. Remaining calm also gives you the clarity of thought that you need to evaluate the situation.

6. Disengage

If the person totally refuses to listen, you have the right to disengage and walk away from the negativity. Say something like 'I'll talk to you later when you calm down.' If you're on your premises, have security escort him out.

7. Avoid violence

In worst-case scenario, the person might try to hit or push you. Getaway before you're provoked to fight back. You might have come across that video of a McDonald's employee who was pushed by an aggressive customer, and she then turned and attacked him viciously. She had to be restrained by her colleagues. Interestingly, the court found the customer guilty of starting the aggression. She only acted in self-defense, albeit very fiercely. This is what a moment of provocation can do to you. This can happen even to the calmest among us. Walk away quickly before your senses lead you to fight back. You can involve the police if the case meets the threshold.

8. Evaluate the situation

After the situation has calmed down, evaluate it rationally as you destress. Is there something that you could have differently? Was the person behaving that way out of habit or was it an isolated case? What can be done to avoid such scenarios in the future? If you determine that that particular person is inherently difficult and constantly refuses to reason, you can cut out any further contact. You're no dumping site for people's negativity. Protect your space at all costs.

For every difficult person that you deal with without losing your calm, give yourself a pat on the back. A lesson well-learned and practiced; right? As long as you remain grounded, you emerge as the bigger person. Remember the aggressor will also be evaluating the incident later. They'll most likely feel embarrassed that they were causing all the trouble while you managed to keep calm.

Can difficult people change? Yes, they can. Yes, they should. If you're willing to help, try to seek them out when they're in a good mood. Speak to them about their attitude and actions. They might see some sense. Give them time to go and reflect, and hopefully, they will change with time.

Chapter 10: Dealing with a Skeptic

Skeptics always doubt and question the ideas others put across. They constantly question opinions when they've already been accepted by the majority. Skeptics want proof that the idea is going to work, or a product is going to function as anticipated, or the projections are going to be achieved, and so on.

Communicating with a skeptic wears you out. You don't want somebody who is constantly poking holes in all your ideas. This is far from constructive criticism, which involves pointing out the weak areas and suggestions on how to improve them. Skeptics simply refuse to believe, often without giving a tangible reason.

Skepticism is most difficult to work within the workplace. With a skeptic in your team, you'll hardly get anything done. The arguments go back and forth, wasting time, and not achieving much. What can you do about this?

1. Question

Skeptics are vague in expressing their doubts. 'I just don't like it.' 'The concept doesn't feel right.' 'What if it doesn't work?' Put them to the task of explaining exactly what they're uncomfortable with. 'What exactly don't you like about the concept?' Chances are they'll struggle to answer that. In the process, they'll become conscious of their tendency to question just for the sake of it. Ask them for alternative suggestions. That shifts their mind from questioning to critical thinking. This applies to teamwork, where you're in a group trying to develop an idea. If you encounter such questions when trying to make a sale, seek to know exactly what the prospective buyer is uncomfortable with. They still may not purchase the product, but should they have a legitimate concern, you can take it up and do something about it.

2. Constructive criticism

When working in a team, let there be a specific time for productive criticism. Let the participants know that you can't just barge in and discredit other people's ideas. Don't interrupt the speaker. Wait for your turn. Have an order of presenting ideas: you can start with presentations, then questions, then open the floor for productive criticism.

Every member of the team must use respectful language. One of the ways to achieve this is to use 'I' instead of 'you.' For instance, imagine saying, 'how can you expect the management to approve such a high budget?' Sounds like an accusation, right? But you can say, 'I don't think the management will approve such a high budget.' Exact the same meaning, yet the second one sounds rational and productive. Encourage constructive criticism even when dealing with skeptic clients. 'What don't you like about the product? What improvements would you like to see? What feature can we add?' such questions should help you pinpoint the reasons for their discontent, which can then give you actionable ideas.

3. Use data

Numbers don't lie. Back up your ideas with numbers whenever applicable. Organize your numbers in a manner that is easy to understand. If you're talking about sales in relation to the marketing budget, break them down into monthly results. Include visual aids such as graphs and charts. Let's say you're making such a presentation as a proposal to increase the marketing budget. With such precise numbers, dealing with skeptics will be easier. All you have to do is challenge them with the data. Should they have doubts, they should also present data to demonstrate their point.

4. Add details

Explain everything, including the questions they may have. In fact when preparing to make such a presentation, have the first draft, consider all the questions that arise from that, then include that information in the second draft.

It is not enough to say to a skeptic that 'these pills will help you lose weight.' You have to add more. Come up with something like 'these pills will help you lose 5 pounds within the first month and up to 7 pounds every month after that without dieting. The pills have no side effects.' You can't afford to be sketchy. Cover all the details that you can think of.

5. Call them aside

Have a separate conversation with these skeptics in your team. There are those who are not even conscious of their attitude. They simply think it's their way of contributing to the team. Others are fully aware of their skeptic selves, and get a kick out of antagonizing others. There are also those who are lazy and don't come up with ideas and want to invalidate the ideas of those who make an effort. Point it out to them away from the meeting.

Let them recognize and evaluate their attitudes. Where is the negativity stemming from? Are they dissatisfied with their job? Or the team they work with? Or are they just as a skeptic in other areas of their lives? Point out the harm done by their attitude to the rest of the team. Encourage them to use constructive criticism instead.

6. Nurture positivity in the organization

Set an optimistic standard in the company. This means that the minds of your workers will be focused on the positive in every situation. Instead of pointing out what won't work, they'll point out what will. Instead of doubting ideas, they'll try to build on them and offer solutions. Let them learn diplomatic dialogue, so that they can learn to express their reservations without affecting the cohesion of the team.

7. In social circles

Cynical people are not just in work circles. You will also encounter them among your friends, family, and community. Unlike the workplace where you have to come to a common agreement so that you can execute, out there you don't always have to agree. Imagine telling your peers about a project that you have in mind, and they're skeptical about it. You're not even telling them to get involved. You're just speaking your idea out loud. Here you can simply agree to disagree. You say it can work. They say it can't work. Your views are different from theirs, and that's fine. You can live and let live.

8. Skeptic crowd

It is possible for a crowd to be cynical due to various reasons. This is an audience that assumes it already knows what you want to say, and already doubts it. This is common in politics. Some candidates are dismissed even before they state their case, mostly if they're from minority groups. If you find yourself in such a situation, acknowledge the skepticism and address it. Say something like, 'you may be wondering what an immigrant could possibly offer this county as a governor..' By stating what is on their minds, you capture their attention and they look up to hear your reply.

There will always be skeptics and pessimists in our midst. Whether at the workplace, in business, school or even in our families. It's important to note, in dealing with such people, one person's definition of success differs from ours and that's fine. The best we can do is be an inspiration, and really understand that we cannot please everybody. Radiate positive vibe for a harmonious co-existence.

Don't write off the skeptical people that you come across. You will definitely need to put in some work before they believe in you, but with the above tips, you can do it. Once they cross that line, you can be assured of their unwavering loyalty.

What if you're the skeptic one? Do you find yourself always second-guessing things that others have already agreed with? Well, you could be a victim. You should be alarmed your conversations always turn to arguments about the merits and demerits of the idea. You should also be alarmed if no one wants to have you in their team. Evaluate the source of your skepticism. Do you have valid reservations, or do you just argue for the sake of it? Imagine how that would feel if you were on the receiving end. You wouldn't like it, right? Make a point of changing your perspective so that you can improve your conversation skills and strengthen your relationships.

Chapter 11: Listening Without Judgment

How often do you listen without forming an opinion on what is being said? We often do it subconsciously and has largely become a habit over time. When you're so quick to judge, you discourage people from speaking to you. Nobody wants to open up on the issues they're dealing with only to receive additional bashing.

If you're in a position of leadership, non-judgmental listening encourages honesty among your subordinates. They'll not be afraid to express their honest views about the organization, and you can then take the appropriate steps to address the issue. Here are some guidelines to help you nurture non-judgmental listening.

1. Mindful listening

We're so accustomed to half-listening, where we're only concentrating partially, while concurrently thinking of what to reply. Mindfulness involves focusing only on the current moment while keeping all other thoughts at bay.

Listen to understand, not to reply. Observe the body language as well. Notice the facial expressions, gestures and so on. Maintain eye contact and nod along the way. The speaker will feel valued and cared for and will be encouraged to share the whole information.

Ever wondered how some counselors easily get people to open up about issues they've kept to themselves for years? This is it. When your listener offers you undivided attention devoid of judgment, your heart just opens up. In a world so used to multitasking, such listening is rare. Setting yourself apart as a mindful listener will be a welcome gift to everyone you come across.

2. Restate

To avoid a monologue, you have to inject once in a while, right? This is mostly where judgmental statements come in, albeit unintentionally.

Let's say that you're listening to someone that lost money in a con game. According to what you're hearing, the signs were so obvious. You're itching to interject and say something like; 'How could you trust people who do not even have an office?' You can hardly think of something positive to say at the moment, especially when the story is still ongoing. Here, you can simply restate what has been said, in different words. You can say something like, 'So you were convinced that it was a legitimate online company?' This reassures the speaker that you're paying keen attention, and encourages the conversation to keep going.

3. Restrain your thoughts

People have a natural tendency toward judgment. You hardly even realize that you're doing something potentially hurtful. You already have set notions on how people should behave in various situations. Anything different is labeled wrong from the onset, if you listen with such an attitude, not much will be achieved.

Be conscious of your thoughts, so you can catch them whenever they turn away from the conversation. Instead of labeling actions as right or wrong, seek to know the circumstances leading there. Ask questions like, 'How did you arrive at that decision?' 'How did that make you feel?' The answers will help you understand the context of the speaker and the reason why some decisions were taken.

4. See things their way

Non-judgmental listening encourages empathy, where you put yourself in the shoes of the listener and feel the emotions. Picture listening to a 20-year-old who is pregnant and the boyfriend has left her. From your point of view, it is easy to wonder how she fell for such a common mistake. *What's wrong with these young girls? Couldn't she wait until she was married? Or at least use contraceptives?*

That's your narrative. But what's her story? She met someone she truly loved. Basically, he looked responsible enough to start a family. She was certain that they would eventually get married. She had always looked forward to being a mother anyway. She then made her decision on the backdrop of these assumptions. As soon as you look at the situation from that angle, you can feel her pain of betrayal, and guide her appropriately.

Sharing a perspective can be challenging when you're dealing with people junior to you; whether in age, status or rank. Their concerns can sound so trivial: A teenager grumbling about an acne breakout, or not having a date for the prom. A college student may start complaining about the lecturers. You may hear a first-time parent complaining about the baby's erratic sleeping schedule or a junior worker complaining about the stress of the job.

If you allow yourself to trivialize their issues from your point of view, you'll be quick to assert how many others have gone through those situations before. Chances are they've already heard that before. And most importantly, it does not make their pain any less. Stepping into their shoes allows you to empathize with your situation, no matter how minor.

5. Silence is fine

You don't always have to interject with an opinion. There are plenty of people who are seeking just to be listened to and not necessarily offered a solution. As we have discussed, your contribution can be simply restating what the speaker said, to demonstrate that you're listening keenly. You can also ask further questions to better understand the issues.

Spare your opinion where it's not required. Silence is also an option. A careful silence that should not be mistaken for loss of interest. Take time to reflect on what the speaker just said. Depending on the intensity of the issues, the silence can take several minutes as the information sinks in. The speaker also uses that moment of silence to catch a breath. Opening up, especially on sensitive matters, takes a lot of energy.

Ask a follow-up question when you're ready to proceed with the conversation. Intermittent periods of silence are healthy. You must have heard that a problem shared is half solved. By listening attentively, you've already made a contribution even before you say anything.

6. Bring out the positives

This applies when dealing with a person who is going through a rough patch. Such a person will be feeling miserable, and it will be difficult to see any good that can come out of the situation. Looking from the outside in, you may be in a position to point out some positives.

Picture speaking to someone who is going through a divorce. All they feel is the misery of a failed marriage. No matter whose fault it was, the pain is not any less. You can point out that separation is an opportunity to start afresh and to first take time for reflection and decide what, if anything, needs to change or apply lessons learned in future relationships as well as to be more cautious when choosing a partner. Bringing out these positive future possibilities will help the person look at the whole situation from a different angle.

Somebody said that if each one of us had that one friend that listens without judgment, the world wouldn't need psychiatrists. Such is the power of non-judgmental listening. In a world that is so quick to judge, you can be that friend.

Chapter 12: Anger Management

Everyone gets angry every once in a while. The problem is not the emotion, but what you do with it. Some manage to stay calm and collected. Others explode into fits of anger. There are several measures that you can take to control your anger. Most of them are long-term. Let us begin by looking at some of the things you can do at that exact moment when emotions are running high. This is important so that you can prevent yourself from saying or doing things that will only aggravate the situation. The quickest thing you can do at the heat of the moment is to try a relaxation technique. Here is a couple that is within reach:

1. Deep Breathing

Simple yet powerful; deep breathing offers instant relief to anger. A surge of anger causes you to take quick, shallow gasps of air. This reduces the supply of oxygen in your bloodstream causing muscle tension. This is the reason an angry person will subconsciously clench the muscles, mainly the abs. The deep breathing relaxation technique aims to draw more air into your body which slows down the heart rate and relaxes the muscles. Take a long, slow breath commonly referred to as belly or abdominal breathing. Let the air fill your chest and belly, hold for a couple of seconds, then breathe out. As you concentrate on your breathing, the emotions will subside.

2. Visualization

Imagine yourself in a beautiful, relaxing and calm place, whether real or just a figment of your imagination. Close your eyes and picture yourself lying on the beach, for instance. Let all your senses come to life. What do you see, hear, smell or touch?

Think of the expanse of blue water stretching as far as your eyes can see. Think of the sound of the crashing waves. Smell the mix of the seawater and the enticing aroma of food coming from the restaurant nearby. Feel your bare feet sink into the sand, and your body absorbing the warmth of the sun. Such vivid visualization lets your mind and body experience the sensation of being in a different place where the anger has no control over you.

3. Progressive Muscle Relaxation

This technique helps you deal with the muscle tension that grips you as your temper rises. Here's how it's done: focus on one muscle group at a time. Start with something as simple as the fist. Tighten your fist for a couple of seconds then release, repeating as necessary. Your hand should feel lighter and more relaxed.

Repeat the same for your feet, thighs, shoulders and so on. Take the neck as far as it can go on each side. Feel the difference? As the tension melts away from your muscles, the anger goes along with it.

4. Music Therapy

Music, the right kind of music, has an instant calming effect on the mind. Fortunately, you can carry music anywhere. Keep your earphones close. Collect inspirational and uplifting music and have it nearby. Every time you feel the emotions rising, you can pop in a tune and soak in the beautiful words and melodies.

These remedies are effective, but only temporary. Eventually, it is advisable to make an effort to deal with your anger for good. Sample the following tips to help you manage your anger in the long term:

1. Shift your thought patterns

When you're angry, everything is painted with a brush of negativity. You can reframe your thinking and replace the negative thoughts and emotions with positive thinking. For instance, instead of thinking that everything is ruined, you are able to comfort yourself; it not the end of the world after all. One of the major strategies that you can use to reframe your thinking is simply thinking logically. Even when sometimes the anger may be justified, it tends to make you become irrational. Remind yourself that the world isn't against you. Treat isolated negative incidences as just that. Bad things do happen to good people. Don't let one unfortunate incident ruin your day.

2. Communicate better

What comes out of your mouth in that moment of anger? Most people yell obscenities and threats - granted it is difficult to control what you say at that moment. How about you don't say anything at all? Silence is definitely an option. It will not be easy when boiling inside, but you'll be glad you did. Speak out when the moment has passed. By then you'll be calm and in a position to express yourself rationally.

 If the aggressor has already gone, let them. This is mostly the case with strangers. Like one who cuts you rudely in traffic, or slides into the parking spot that you've been waiting for. You might be tempted to give such fellows a piece of your mind, reasoning that by the time the anger subsides, they would have left. What will this achieve? Nothing. If anything they could make matters worse by cursing right back, and before you know it you're in each other's faces. These scenarios don't end well. Let the jerks go, they'll meet their match.

3. Take a break

When a situation is getting stressful, take a break. There is a recent viral video where a man steps out of his car in standstill traffic and begins to dance. He dances like there's nobody watching, yet hundreds are. Perhaps this is his version is taking a break instead of sitting in the car and dealing with the frustrations of getting late.

You too can take a break. Maybe you're in a tense meeting and you can feel the emotions rising. Ask for a break and walk around the block. Those minutes that you take to breath and calm down will prevent you from getting angry when things heat up.

Arguing with your partner? Leave the house. This is not that kind of arrogant leaving where you bang doors. No. Leave calmly and go take a walk. Take the dog with you if you may. The sights, sounds, and scents of the outdoors are therapy in themselves. By the time you get back house, you'll be composed enough for a reasonable discussion.

If you can slot in exercise, even better - jogging, running, working out, yoga and so on. Physical exercise releases feel-good hormones that counter the anger.

4. Identify Triggers

What flares your temper? Is it the boss talking down at you? Or your colleagues teasing you? Or your spouse nagging you yet again? Or is it the strangers who still have some manners to learn? Think of how to deal with the situation beforehand. Play the scenario in your mind and evaluate the best way to react to each one.

When the teasing begins, you can shut them out by playing music on your earphones. You can agree with your spouse to set aside time for resolving conflicts so that they don't have to pop up anyhow. Identifying the triggers of your anger helps get ready for them so they don't overwhelm you.

Explore the contributing factors

Anger issues can be triggered by the things one experienced in their upbringing. If there was violence in the family, with members expressing their anger by hitting each other, screaming and throwing things around, and therefore you think that is the way to express anger. Highly stressful and traumatic events make one more susceptible to anger too. Here you have to deal with the underlying issue and in the process reduce your vulnerability to anger.

Nobody enjoys being angry. It is an emotion that takes over you and leads you to say and do things you didn't even think you're capable of. You don't have to suffer at the mercy of your temper. These tips should help you put it under control. If you're still struggling with fits of fury after this, you can get professional help.

Chapter 13: Iron the Tension: Using Irony to Navigate Difficult Situations

Irony refers to a figure of speech where you say something that is the opposite of reality. Irony pokes fun at situations for humor. For instance, a speaker walking into a meeting that is so scarcely attended muses, 'oh, what a mammoth crowd we have here!'

You'd have expected that the speaker will first stand there for a moment of disappointed silence or there would be uncomfortable whispering between him and the organizers of the event. He would then go-ahead to speak grudgingly. However, with that ironic statement, all that is ironed away. The audience chuckles at the joke. Their spirits are already lifted. They can tell that the speaker will not be any less enthusiastic because of the numbers. And just like that, the situation is salvaged.

The irony is different from sarcasm. One is often mistaken for the other, and in some quarters the terms are used interchangeably. However, there is a distinct difference between them. While irony seeks to poke fun, sarcasm mostly criticizes the situation or person.

When trying to have a rational conversation, sarcasm is discouraged. It may invite some giggles, but the teasing and insults can be demoralizing to most people. Here are some examples of what sarcastic comments can sound like:

- This steak is as soft as a leather boot.
- Seems you didn't let education interfere with your ignorance.
- Keep talking. I yawn when I'm interested.
- You're sharp. But that's just my opinion, unlike hundreds of others.
- Consider doing some soul searching. You might be lucky enough to find one.

These comments are funny when you hear them in a movie. If they're directed to you, they sting. They ridicule your effort, expertise, and intelligence.

The irony is a safer bet. It is always advisable to direct the irony to a situation as opposed to a person. It may sound like harmless fun to you, but the listener hears something different.

Alternatively, you can direct the ironic statement to yourself, a form of self-deprecating humor.

Picture a staff meeting in a company that has had a loss-making year. The situation is definitely tense. The employees don't know what the boss will say. He finally comes in, and they sit nervously, avoiding his eyes as he peruses the report. Then he finally chimes in, 'oh, see what we have here. Hello Fortune 5oo!' The room is engulfed in chuckles. The tension is dissipated. From there, the team can embark on a rational discussion regarding the measures that need to be taken.

Notice that the irony is not directed to anyone in particular. It pokes fun at the situation. It eliminates the chances of leaving anyone feeling offended or belittled. This is very crucial. Even in navigating difficult situations, do not do it at the expense of other's feelings.

By now you should have your own ideas of situations where a dash of irony could have helped stabilize the situation. The irony is not a solution, but it lifts the tension so that you can then think of a solution with clarity.

Chapter 14: Use Laughter to Lighten the Conversation

Throwing in a joke or two or a bunch into a conversation makes it a lot lighter, dissipates tension and gets the listeners glued. Whether it's a corporate talk or a casual conversation, the funny fellow always gets the audience.

Some people are naturally funny, others not quite. If you fall into the second category, as most people do, you can learn to be funny. You're not trying to be a comedian; the goal here is to use humor strategically to make the conversation interesting.

The now popular memes across the internet clearly demonstrate our affinity for humor. Serious messages are coded in-jokes, and you can't help laugh them off. Even the president is not spared. In fact, President Donald Trump has always been a subject of memes. Put in any other way, this information could be regarded as defamation. But throw in some humor and you can get away with it, and we all get a good laugh while at it. Here are some guidelines in developing and using humor in your conversations.

1. Use it to diffuse tension

Former President Abraham Lincoln was once accused of being 'two-faced' by his opponent. Knowing the nature of politicians, this could have quickly degenerated into a verbal confrontation that could have gone on and on. Instead, the president simply quipped, 'if I had two faces, would I be wearing this one?' It was such an unexpected reply, you bet even the opponent was amused. You can apply similar humor in different situations around you to melt the tension and bring the people back to a rational conversation.

2. What makes people laugh?

This applies when you're not naturally funny and you need to put in some work. First, determine what makes you laugh. When you read or watch shows, what is it that you find funny? Is it the puns, rants or exaggeration? It is easier to develop your humor around what you find funny. Secondly, what is it that you say that gets people laughing even when you didn't intend to be funny? Is it the puns? Try working on those and using them more regularly. Here's the one you can throw in at the office party: 'I was hoping to sneak some leftovers. Seems like my plans have already been foiled.'

3. Humor techniques

They include self-deprecation, exaggeration, puns, wordplay and so on.

Self-deprecation is one of the most common; making fun of yourself. It stands a zero chance of offending others. Like when a speaker with a funny face says something like, 'how can I face the problem if the problem is my face?' This kind of humor tells your audience that you're willing to be vulnerable enough to acknowledge your weaknesses.

The technique should be used in moderation though; too much of it and you begin to sound like you're suffering from low self-esteem. Although make sure that you don't ridicule a part of you that is related to your expertise. For instance, if you're a healthy-living advocate, don't crack jokes on binge eating. Don't give the impression of someone who preaches one thing and takes another.

Exaggeration – The town is so small that the entry and exit signs are on the same pole.

Sarcasm – I can keep a secret. It's the people I tell them who can't.

Pun – The inventor of throat lozenges died last month. There was no coffin at the funeral.

Random – The letter from the lawyer was labeled 'final notice.' Good! He can finally leave us alone.

There are many more humor techniques that you can draw inspiration from. You can even introduce your own. Get people laughing and you can be assured they'll want to keep listening to you.

4. Give the message priority

Don't get too excited about cracking jokes that you forget about your core content. We're using laughter here to lighten the conversation, meaning the main focus is on the conversation. If you're giving a formal presentation where you need to first write down your ideas, you don't have to include the jokes in the first draft. Dedicate the first draft to the message that you want to deliver. You can then weave in the jokes in the second draft.

5. Sound Natural

The jokes should blend seamlessly into the rest of the content. Practice beforehand if you have to. Forced jokes bring in awkward moments at best. Long after you've spoken it, your listener realizes that it was supposed to be a joke. But it wasn't funny. You'll attract a chuckle at best, from a listener or two trying to be courteous. Not good at all for your impression.

Don't introduce a joke either. Just throw it in there like you're not even trying. Don't laugh at your own jokes, and definitely, don't start laughing before you crack the joke. In fact, you should look like you don't even think it's funny.

The opinion is divided on whether you can start a conversation with a joke. Popular televangelist Joel Osteen always starts his sermons with a joke and apparently, it seems to work. Others argue that starting with a joke makes you seem too eager. And should that joke fail, the rest of your conversation is in jeopardy. Here we say if you can come up with a good relevant joke that will blend into the conversation, why not?

6. Avoid ridiculing others

Avoid poking fun directly to your listeners. Something may sound like a joke to you, while someone else hears something completely different. Make fun of things and events, not the people you're talking to. Make fun of your common challenges. It gives people the feeling of 'we're in this together.'

Teasing students over their poor performance, or employees over the company's losing streak, it not motivating them. You're just killing their spirits.

Unintended ridicule can also come in the form of controversial topics such as politics, religion, race, gender, sexuality, and so on. Remember that case in Paris where someone poked fun on Islam, and the next thing they knew retaliatory bombs were ripping buildings apart. With some of these topics, they're no harmless jokes.

Remember to crack just enough jokes, not too many. If you're slotting in a joke after every five sentences, perhaps you should consider comedy. As long as you're engaging in normal conversation, use them only periodically. If you have mastered the art of using jokes to relieve tension, you will be better at conflict management. Take a cue from good old Abraham Lincoln. Get people laughing and the strife is soon forgotten.

Chapter 15: Inclusive Communication; Involving the Interlocutor

The conversation must be two-way, involving speaking and listening for both parties. Don't be a mean speaker, hardly giving the others a chance to chip in. Sometimes, this happens subconsciously. You set out to speak for just a few minutes, but once you kick-off, you find yourself going on and on. How can you hold yourself from a monologue and encourage active participation?

- Sets goals together. Decide where the conversation is headed, and what it's intended to achieve. Is it supposed to come up with solutions to a certain issue? Or an action plan? Or come up with a list? Once you're on the same page regarding what needs to be done, you can be sure there will be active participants in the discussion.

- Kick the conversation into high gear. When you speak first, you set the tone for the discussion. If you start off in a dull and distracted way, it will be difficult to lift the debate from there. The interlocutor could get bored and trail off. Starting on a high note increases interest and improves participation.

- Use open-ended questions as opposed to those that can simply be answered with a yes or no. Instead of asking, 'do you agree with this list?' ask 'what more can we add on this list?' This calls for more detailed answers and ultimately a more comprehensive conversation.

- Ask follow-up questions. For instance, if you're talking about the list above and an interlocutor suggests that you should include political leaders, ask which specific leaders should be included.

- Avoid repeating the same point over and over again, or explaining it at length, in an attempt to get understood. Just explain once then give an opportunity for questions. The questions then determine the direction the conversation should take.

- Have moments of silence where you all reflect on the matters that have been discussed. This is also a time to refresh so you get back into the conversation with fresh energy.

- Avoid having one person steering the conversation all the time. Since you have already agreed on the goal of the conversation, any of you can lead.

Inclusive communication is all about balancing speaking and listening. Communications experts suggest that you should not be speaking for more than 20 seconds. However, this rule is not set on stone. It can apply if you're having a one on one conversation. If you're speaking to a group of people, chances are you'll go on until you've made your point before you allow the next person to contribute. Pay attention to the body language of listeners. If they break eye contact and fidget, you've probably been going on for too long. Break the monopoly with a question. At the end of the day, the objective is to make sure that all parties are given an opportunity to participate in the discussion and make their ideas heard.

Chapter 16: Diplomatic Dialogue

Diplomatic dialogue refers to a situation where you handle a dispute successfully, leaving all parties satisfied, and without causing a fallout. Diplomacy uses persuasion, negotiation, reason, and compassion. These skills are useful in many areas of life, more so in the workplace. Since the workplace brings together many different people from different backgrounds and with different opinions, it is bound to experience disputes every once in a while. Below are some of the features that form a diplomatic dialogue:

1. Listen

You have heard this word so many times now right? We can't help it. Listening is half of communication, so it will come up time and again. In resolving a dispute, all parties must be heard. You can't walk into the room with preconceived notions on who is right or wrong. Let the parties put all the issues on the table. Even where you have a contrary opinion, allow the people to express themselves first. Once you have all the issues out in the open, you can then start the process of evaluating them.

2. No negative words

Rephrasing statements can make a lot of difference. Instead of saying 'that is a lie' say 'that is not true'. Instead of saying 'that is a bad idea' say 'that is not a good idea'. Exact the same meaning, but without using the negative words. Negative words make people angry and defensive. Imagine your boss telling you that 'this report is full of mistakes.' You instantly get angry. You're likely to get into a rant about your work not being appreciated. Even if you don't say it out loud, you'll be spewing the venom in your mind.

Now picture the very same scenario, but the boss says 'this report needs some editing.' Sounds like a bliss right? It almost sounds like a compliment. He's acknowledging that the work is done, it only needs a few modifications. Words have power. Use them carefully and people will be at peace.

3. Sorry

We're often teaching kids to say sorry, yet it seems that even adults can use a bit more of the word. Putting the word sorry in front of a potentially offensive statement makes it much more palatable. For instance, if the debate if going off-topic; you can say 'sorry but I don't think this is the point of discussion here' or 'sorry but I think you're out of order.' Use it when you want to interject a conversation. 'Sorry but I have to say something here.' or 'sorry but I don't agree with what you're saying.

Remove the sorry, and the statement instantly feels aggressive, likely to provoke the recipient into a verbal bout. Use the word generously and let it work its magic in facilitating a diplomatic dialogue.

4. Refer to yourself

Referring to other people always comes across as confrontational. 'You did not send the report on time' sounds like you're spoiling for a fight. Compare that with 'I did not receive the report on time.' Sounds rather harmless, right? You will have the report handed to you without spoiling anyone's day. Instead of saying 'your idea is not clear' say 'I seem not to have understood your idea.' Just a little wordplay and disputes that could have escalated to something ugly are resolved amicably.

What do you gain from diplomatic dialogue in the workplace? The workers will be content with the manner in which conflicts are handled. That will improve relationships between them, resulting in a conducive working environment.

Diplomatic dialogue can be employed at home too. See how you can incorporate the above guidelines when handling disagreements with your spouse or other family members. Then you can be sure of sorting the issues without ruining the relationships.

Chapter 17: Shyness and Social Anxiety

Why is it that some people thrive in social settings while others cringe just at the thought of it? Shyness and social anxiety can be traced back to past experiences, exposure and personality traits.

Shy people avoid social gatherings and will be in the furthest corner of the room if they have to be there. They'll arrive last, and leave first. While that is harmless on the face of it, it keeps you from establishing meaningful relationships in the various areas of your life. You should make conscious steps to deal with social anxiety, as it could escalate into an anxiety disorder which will take therapy to treat.

Shyness is largely a habit that can be unlearnt. Decide that you don't want to live your life in the shadow of anxiety. Sample these steps that you can take:

1. Take action

Shyness is mostly based on unfounded fears. It should not be mistaken with being an introvert. Introverts are not necessarily shy. They may be quiet and reserved, but when the situation calls for it, they can hold conversations without fear.

Shy people are afraid of what people will think about them. What if people don't like me? What if I can't find anything meaningful to say? What if I get embarrassed?

Fear thrives in inaction. As soon as you begin to do something, the fear quickly dissipates. It is an illusion after all. As the famous Dutch painter Vincent Van Gogh put it if a voice within you says that you can't paint, by all means, do, and the voice will be silenced.

What is it that your fear tells you that you cannot do? Speak up in a room full of people? By all means, speak. Make a brief comment, or ask a question. Similarly, pick up a conversation with a stranger. Engage a neighbor that you've never spoken to before. Talk to a colleague about something other than work. The moment may be nerve-wracking, but it will be followed by a feeling of empowerment. You did it! The idea of doing it again will not frighten you as much. With time, you'll be wondering what you were afraid of in the first place.

2. Speak out

Shy people speak a lot; in their minds. For every sentence that they manage to voice out, there are several other racing in the mind. What's the worst that could happen if you actually spoke out? Challenge yourself to do so.

Ask those questions. Ask for clarifications when you've not understood. Raise your concerns. Case in point; your supervisor gives you unclear instructions. You sit there thinking, 'what did he just say?' You try to figure it out yourself, just as you have done many times before. Wait; how about you just ask? Go on, walk into that office and ask.

You sit in a meeting thinking, 'what, we just used that strategy last time and it did not work.' Verbalize your thoughts. Say it. Your voice and ideas deserve to be heard. Don't be preoccupied with what others think of you. Chances are they're not going to scrutinize you half as much as you think. It's all in your mind. Who knows, you could be sitting on the next big idea that the world needs to hear. And it all begins with speaking up.

3. Have a confident body language

Your body communicates even before you get a word out of your mouth. When you walk into a room, you make the first impression even before you start speaking. Let your body language portray confidence. Walk with your head high. Shake hands firmly. Maintain eye contact. Project an audible voice. Maintain comfortably close proximity; don't stand so far like you're just waiting to bolt out of the door. Don't get so near either that you have to speak in a whisper.

When you portray confidence, you feel confident, and act like it. Your listener or audience will have noticed a positive first impression. They will have high expectations of you. This, the perception that others have of you, also affects how you feel and act. If you present a sloppy body language, your listener will not expect much from you. You can tell by the way they look at you without much interest and only give you partial attention. You feel dismissed even before you start talking.

What does this do for your confidence? It just plummets. Everything you do after that will be sloppy, just like they predicted. And their perception of you will have been vindicated. Notice the downward spiral? Make an effort to appear confident even when you don't feel like it. Once you raise the expectations of people, it'll be easier to measure up.

4. Don't label yourself shy

Some people tend to dangle their shyness like it's a pleasant thing. While shyness is not a sin or crime, it can keep you from opportunities when you fail to communicate to those who facilitate them. Your shyness isn't something you should print on a T-shirt. Don't use it to escape responsibilities or give up chances.

Would you like to give a presentation on behalf of the department? *No, I'm shy*. Would you like to hang out in our social club? *I can't, I'm shy*. Would you like to dance? How about you read the family speech at the wedding? Or check out the new neighbors? Same old excuse. *I'm shy; thank you very much*.

Once you refer to yourself as shy, others will pick the Que. Hearing others call you shy will only make the situation worse. If somebody calls you shy, say something to disassociate yourself from the tag. You can say something like, 'I just haven't had the chance to meet people around here' or 'I just wasn't ready for that particular presentation.' Words have power. What you're constantly called, you eventually become.

5. Identify triggers

What triggers your social anxiety? Is it your work station? Or public presentations? What exactly are you afraid of doing in that situation? For instance, why are you shy in your workplace? Are you afraid of being scolded for not doing a good job? Then improve your work ethic. Are your colleagues mean? Surely they can't be all bad. There has to be one, or a number, that you can approach and talk to. Remember what we said about verbalizing your thoughts?

Once you identify the trigger for your anxiety, you can pinpoint the exact thing that you're afraid of. You can then take action to make it better. Practice speaking. Dress well. Master your content. The more prepared you are, the less afraid you'll be.

6. Identify your strengths

Don't dwell too much on what you're not good at, like engaging people in this case. What is it that you do well? Put emphasis on that. In the office for instance, what is it that you're an expert in? Maybe you write the most detailed reports. Or you're a good editor, who can smell a mistake from a mile away. Perhaps you draft the most convincing marketing emails. Hone that expertise. Let your colleagues know you as the go-to person for various tasks. They'll no longer dwell much on your shyness. In any case, being good in one area encourages you to try out something more. For instance, after you've written a flawless report, how about you present it at the meeting? Emboldened by your expertise, you'll be encouraged to put yourself out there more, and step by step you will overcome your shyness.

In a social setting, such as a family gathering, take a similar approach. What is it that you're skilled in? Cooking, for instance. Instead of hanging out there having awkward conversations, get into the kitchen. Churn out those delicacies. From there you will have compliments, and others asking for the recipe. You have a great conversation starter already. Since it's your area of expertise, you'll speak with confidence. Who was that calling you shy again?

7. Practice conversation starters

Starting a conversation is the most nerve-wracking part for shy people. You can think of conversation starters before-hand so you can have them close. Complements work magic. Say something nice about someone's outfit, haircut, perfume or even skill. A complement lifts up the spirit of the listener and makes him/her more receptive to the conversation.

Making an inquiry is also a great way to break the ice. *Where can I get a taxi around here? Do you know of any fitness clubs that I can join? Would you know if the lecturer gave an assignment last week?* Such queries make people feel knowledgeable and useful. Notice that you're not asking for much; just information. Even if the listener does not have the correct response, you can both pick up a conversation on how to get the information.

Remember once you get a conversation going, you need to get it going. Keep yourself updated with issues of interest so you can have content for conversation. The ability to throw in an intelligent remark on any given subject will go a long way to keep the dialogue going.

These tips should help you ease away from shyness toward confidence. There may still be those moments where you're trying to join a conversation but you're tongue-tied. Do not let that one moment ruin your entire day. Keep taking small steps towards confident communication, and don't stop until your voice is heard.

Chapter 18: Productive Conflict

Can anything good come out of conflict? The answer is a definite yes. The secret lies in the resolving of the conflict. Dealing with conflict is no mean task. At the workplace, many managers struggle with or even avoid the process. It is assumed that disagreements always leave behind a trail of destruction. While this is sometimes the case; they don't have to. You can resolve conflict in 2 capacities. One, where you're not directly involved with the conflict and are only coming in as a mediator. Secondly, you can be part of the conflict, who is facing the other party to attempt to talk out things between them. Either way, here's how to handle conflict and turn it into something positive:

1. Calm down and reflect

This applies in face-to-face, confrontational instances. Very little can be achieved in the heat of the moment, when emotions are running high. Tempers are likely to be flaring, and words are thrown around. In the worst-case scenario, the situation can escalate into physical violence. The solution here is to getaway. The longer you are in each other's faces, the higher the chances of things going south. People say things they don't mean when they're mad. You know that once words go forth, there's no taking them back. Apologies may be said later, but the emotional damage done could last a lifetime.

Let's say that you're the mediator here. For instance, you're a teacher, and two students come running to you after a confrontation. They're both yelling in an attempt to explain to you what happened and to exonerate themselves from blame. You don't have to handle all the shouting. Send them back to class, with a strict warning to cease the confrontation, and tell them to return to your office the following day. The demeanor will be totally different then, and you can have a rational conversation.

2. Empathy

Empathetic listening involves going beyond the words to feel the emotions of the speaker. If you're facing your aggressor, chances are you're coming to the table with an 'I am right attitude.' If the other party does the same, neither of you will be listening. Take a moment and put yourself in the shoes of the interlocutor. Listen. This is not easy to do in times of arguments. Maintain eye contact, or at least try. Think of the circumstances that could have led to various decisions and actions. If you think about it reasonably, perhaps you'd have reacted the same way. Or maybe you can agree that there was justified cause to react that way.

As an intermediary, you're even better placed to listen since you're not emotionally invested in the situation. Listen to both parties then state your understanding of the situation. You should be the sounding board for both parties. Help them see each other's perspectives. If you're dealing with your subordinates at work, remind them of the company values. You're not looking for a winner and loser; it's not a competition. Discuss measures to avoid such conflicts in the future.

3. Express, forgive and ask for forgiveness

What is your side of the story? Explain what happened, the emotions you went through, your perception of the situation and the circumstances that lead to the decisions that you made. Let the interlocutor do the same. If you happen to turn out to be on the wrong, accept it. Everyone makes mistakes. You're no exception. It is not easy to say sorry when you came to the discussion table all ready to be vindicated, but it is necessary. Forgive even as you're forgiven. Carrying the burden of forgiveness will only prolong the conflict unnecessarily. Forgiveness also helps foster cohesion so you can continue to work as a team.

4. Speak of yourself

A simple play of words changes the conversation from confrontational to rational. 'You did not copy me on that email.' Sounds accusing at best, and sends the listener to the defense. If you say 'I was not copied on that email' you sound calmer. You're not really accusing anyone, although the culprit is obvious. The two sentences have the exact same meaning, yet the second one allows for a more reasonable discussion.

This works even with couples. 'You don't appreciate me' sounds so much worse compared to 'I don't feel appreciated.' The first version is likely to attract defense, while the second one attracts empathy.

Also, be careful when using 'always' and 'never.' 'You never contribute to team projects/you're never there for us/you never listen, etc. Or you always undermine my ideas/you always come late/you always side with my opponent. Such generalizations hurt. Surely there's no one person who does the wrong thing all the time. Insinuating so only makes the conflict worse. Restrict yourself to the particular issues at hand.

5. Initiate reconciliation

Conflicts can simmer on for days, months or even years without anyone taking any initiative to resolve them. Often, the opponents are too proud to seek dialogue. They result in using the silent treatment as a weapon. It becomes a silent competition. Neither of them wants to speak first. The first to speak 'lose.' This is common, especially in relationships.

Unfortunately, silence solves nothing. All that time you're wasting in silence could be spent doing productive things together. But pride keeps you from utilizing those moments. Isn't your relationship more important to you than your ego?

6. Be flexible

Be ready to accommodate the views of others, even as they accommodate yours. Hardline stands only fuel the disagreement. Imagine a couple arguing about the husband coming home late. One of the most common arguments in the world; right? The wife insists that the husband must be home on time for dinner with the family every night. In her opinion, that is the right thing to do. Family dinners are important bonding times that should be upheld at all costs.

What is the opinion of the husband? That he needs to catch up with the boys after work. They watch sport and chat over a drink. 'How will I have a social life if I don't get to go anywhere after work?'

Who needs to be flexible here? Ideally, both of them. They can agree that the husband can go out after work, but only for 3 nights a week. If either of them maintains their rigid stands, the conflict will only get worse.

When there's an argument in any situation, you have the 2 parties in separate ends. If each of them can take a few steps towards the centerline, the disparity gets nearer to being resolved.

7. Remember your common goal

If you've been interacting enough to get into a conflict, you must have a common interest. If you work for the same company, then your objective is to advance the vision of the company. That is where you're all working towards. You're headed in the same direction after all. You may not agree on the particulars of the journey, but you have a similar destination.

Conflict does not have to be destructive. You can learn a lot from those unpleasant encounters. Often, those you disagreed with the turn out to be your greatest friends. Disagreements come and go, and those who know how to handle them that remain standing.

Chapter 19: Honing Your Personality for Business Success

What comes to mind when you think of starting and running a business? Money; right? From a layman's point of view; money rules. However, as exemplified by top entrepreneurs across the world, there's so much that comes before money. Your personality is one of the key aspects that determine your success in business. Sample these personality traits that set you up for success in business; how many of them do you possess?

1. Passionate

It has been famously said that if you love what you do, you won't have to work for a day in your life. This tells you that you should be cautious when choosing your line of business. You may be tempted to go into the sector that is doing well at the moment. Or a business that your acquaintance went into and made good money. But remember before the money, you will have to put in the hours. It only makes sense then that you choose what you like. Many expert chefs, bakers, fashion designers, hairdressers, and programmers were drawn into their line of business by passion. Their motivation was to create something great. In return, a lot of people liked their work and were willing to pay for it, and before they knew it they were dollar millionaires. Let your interests lead you to your path of business, and your working days will be well behind you.

2. Strong people skills

Relationships are essential in every area of our lives, and business is no exception. The ability to communicate and relate with people has a direct positive impact on your business. Keith Ferrazzi; CEO of Ferazzi Greenlight and the author of business relationships handbooks *Never Eat Alone* and *Who's Got your Back?* Emphasizes the need for strong people skills in business. He attributes the success of world-class entrepreneurs to 'the number, quality, and depth of their social capital.' Social capital here refers to the relationships they establish with their workers, partners, suppliers, financiers, and clients. Strive Masiyiwa, the founder of Econet Group says that in business, you should always endeavor to form relationships even before you need them. Research has shown that one of the common factors among successful business leaders is their ability to connect with people. Your social capital will form the basis of your business.

3. Trustworthy

Honestly is of the essence in business. People need to know that they can trust you; you will keep your word. Most successful entrepreneurs are fiercely trustworthy, people require their signatures only for formal purposes.

In business, it is often tempting to cut corners to save operational costs. Businessmen start off well, giving the market quality products so as to attract customers. With time, they get clever or impatient. Maybe they're not selling as much as they projected. We have goods on sale that do not have half the ingredients indicated on the label. We also have gadgets that are seriously underwhelming if their adverts are anything to go by. Cutting corners only takes you too far. Remember an unhappy customer tells tens of others. The little money you save cutting the corners could be nothing compared to the clients you lose in the long term.

Being honest with your employees, suppliers, financiers, and partners ensures that they stick by you. Make your payments on time. Should something go wrong and you can't keep your word, communicate the same in good time. They're human; they'll understand. And they'll appreciate that you value them enough to keep them in the loop.

4. Self-motivation

Unlike in employment, once you start your own business, you don't have a boss breathing down your neck. You have to motivate yourself. This is not a problem at the beginning. At the start of a new business, you have all the gusto in the world. You're excited. You have your company vision, mission, and projections somewhere in your wallet, where you look at them often. And smile.

With time, things get bumpy. No matter how well prepared you thought you were, business teaches you that some of these lessons are only learned through experiences. You may be having a difficult time getting people as excited as you are about new products and ideas. Maybe the sales are way below par or you no longer see eye to eye with your partner. The employees, you could have sworn you had the best pick, apparently not quite.

You begin to struggle to get out of bed. The impetus seems to be drying up. That is where self-motivation comes in. You have to keep reminding yourself of the reason why you started and the vision you had at the beginning. So you continue to wake up when you feel like it and when you don't. Without self-motivation, the business does not go far.

5. Goal-oriented

Successful businessmen don't just shoot; they have a clear image of the target. Setting and achieving goals is at the core of entrepreneurship. The goals here must be SMART:

Specific – The goal should be stated in very precise terms. Not just something like 'increase our sales'. You must state the exact numbers that you target to reach.

Measurable – Here you need to include numbers so that at any one time you're able to calculate the progress.

Attainable – You may be drawing your inspiration from Fortune 500 companies, but you still need to make your goals realistic. If you set them too high you're unlikely to hit them, and have will leave you de-energized.

Relevant- Tie the goals to the vision and mission of your business. They must be geared towards strengthening the core values of the company.

Time-bound – You must specify the duration during which these objectives should be achieved. It is not enough to target increased sales. Include a timeline. 'Increase sales by 20% in the next month.

6. Risk-taker

Business is not for the faint-hearted. Quite often, things do not go as expected. You don't have much of a safety net as you do in employment. You have to be bold enough to decide that you want to plunge in there never the less. Most successful entrepreneurs, such as Richard Branson of the Virgin Group, have failed a good number of times before they tasted lasting success. They have been auctioned, declared bankrupt and sold failing businesses just to provide basics for their families. Yet at the end of it all, they go right back and try again, with no guarantee of success. If you're such a risk-taker, you have a higher chance of ending up with a successful business.

7. Discipline

Many successful entrepreneurs follow a strict routine, often with no supervision. Can you establish a routine and stick to it? Can you, for instance, go for a morning run every day at 5 am? Or go to the gym twice a week? Or have your financial records ready by the 3rd of every month?

Remember you're not under supervision here. You're the boss. There'll be mornings that you'd rather sleep a little more. Or days when you're so tired that even the thought of the gym drains you. So what if the records are not ready by the 3rd? 5th or 6th will do just fine, right?

Maintaining discipline in the absence of supervision is an ability a few possess. If you can hack it, you're a step closer to running a profitable business.

There you have it. By now you must have gauged yourself to see where you stand in the personality test. Some of these traits are inborn. Those that you don't have; you can develop and nurture. Create your unique personality and increase the chances of attaining your dream of running a business.

Chapter 20: The Art of Persuasion

Persuasion involves influencing others to see your point of view. People who have mastered the art of persuasion easily rise to leadership positions. Why? People listen to them, trust them and follow them. In business, persuasion will get you partners, financiers and most importantly, clients. Expert persuaders make great marketers. Persuasion skills come in handy in every area of life. You have ideas that deserve to be heard, and your ability to convince others is your first step to getting them implemented.

1. Get interested

Take the time to study your subjects. Who are they? What do they like? What challenges do they face? What solutions are they looking for? Whether you're selling a house, organizing a company team-building or trying to convince the neighbors to form a community welfare group, you have to show interest in the people first. It flatters people when you show concern for the issues affecting them. They grow to like and trust you. They're convinced that any ideas that you come up with are for their good, and you'll find it easy to influence them.

2. Give before you take

People are prone to reciprocating favors done to them. Like the biblically-stated giving, it often comes back in good measure, pressed and running over. Adam Grant is an author, psychologist and University of Pennsylvania lecturer. In his book *Give and Take*, he documents research that demonstrates that people who constantly help others achieve more success in the long run.

The giving here does not have to be monetary. You can give time, advise, support or information. This notion is often exemplified in company websites. Let's say you're looking for a weight loss product. You land on one website which simply gives you a list of their products plus the benefits.

The second website first gives you information about your weight. It offers you a free calculator where you calculate your Body Mass Index. It offers an explanation of what BMI means in relation to your weight and overall health. It gives you information on factors affecting your weight: age, lifestyle, diet and so on. All this material is offered to you before you part with a single cent.

Which website will you buy from? The choice is obvious. Even if you don't buy immediately, you will bookmark the site for when you're ready to make a purchase. You're also likely to subscribe so that any new information does not pass you by.

When you give, you make people feel valued and appreciated. When you then ask something from them, whether it's to make a purchase or join a certain cause, they'll be more than ready to reciprocate. Such is the power of giving before asking to receive.

3. Personalize the message

Consider your audience in phrasing your message. The way you address college students must be different from the way you address senior citizens. You may also have to modify the different genders.

Let us use the example of health products once again; weight loss products to be precise. When introducing such products to women, you can emphasize the need to look good in cute dresses, avoid stretch marks, acquire a bikini body and so on. These are issues that are close to their hearts.

Men may not respond as effectively to a message phrased as such. The word 'fat' seems not to sound as atrocious to men as it does to women. If the old clothes don't fit, how about just get others a size (or 3) larger? And don't even get started about the beach. They'll comfortably spot their beer bellies, shirtless, and enjoy their holiday without a care in the world. They insert 'big' before their name and actually make it sound cool. Thank you very much, Big Austin.

See? A message that was well-received by the women goes in and out for the men. Perhaps the way to get men to listen in this case would be to hit below the belt, quite literally. Tie your products to sexual health. Sexual prowess, to be exact. The idea that they can be beasts (or close) in bed can get them eating oats and celery sticks in no time. Or whatever else you suggest.

If you're speaking to a creative, such as an artist, do not drown them in analytical figures. Spare that for the business executives. These ones are fascinated by numbers, they say they don't lie. Creatives thrive in hearing how ideas will come to life.

You must carefully choose which detail to exemplify depending on whom you're speaking to. These are just a few examples of personalizing the message depending on the receiver. The principal goes beyond the business world to other facets of life. You should now be in a position to do the same depending on your situation.

4. Persistence

When people do not positively receive your message right away, you have to be prepared to say it time and again. Sounds like nagging, right? Not necessarily. Think of politicians campaigning for political posts. They campaign for months, speaking to people every day, essentially repeating the same message over and over. Should they lose that particular election, they return the following one and continue expounding the reasons they believe they're best placed to represent the people. Former President Abraham Lincoln lost 8 separate elections before he was elected to the highest office in the land.

There is something about a man (or woman) who asks without ceasing. One who refuses to back down. The persistence convinces people that he has ideas that will make an impact on their lives. Even the most stubborn of them end up listening.

How can you remain persistent without being a nuisance? Keep paraphrasing the message. Say things differently. Add some more details each time. Develop a demo or prototype. Collect relevant statistics. People respond better to something they can see as opposed to plain words. Give the listeners time to process the information, then communicate again. Keep knocking on that door, and eventually, it'll be opened one way or the other.

5. Confidence

To make others see your point of view, you have to communicate with conviction. Your verbal and body language makes the first impression and determines the perception of the listener towards you. Whether you're giving a speech, speaking to a small group of people or to a single person, confidence is key.

How do you portray confidence? Body language first. Walk with your head high. Maintain steady eye contact. Shake hands firmly. This will make people want to hear what you have to say. Listen attentively when it's the listeners turn to speak. Nod periodically.

Confidence carries an aura of energy that is instantly transferred to others. It motivates and excites them about your ideas. They can see that you're totally sold on the idea, and this will increase their curiosity and make them want to try it.

6. Sense of urgency

Make your listener see that there is a limited time. This is a strategy mostly used in marketing. What do they tell you? Hurry while stocks last! Offer valid for the first 100 buyers! Buy today and get a discount! In most of these sales, the stock is not limited as they want to make you believe. They know a sense of urgency works. They manage to convince you that it'll be a privilege to be among the first buyers and receive a certain offer. And it works.

Still, on marketing matters, make sure you demonstrate that other people have shown interest or given good reviews of your ideas. In this age of social media, you can rely on the response that you're getting online as proof of interest.

Begin by posting your idea online on multiple platforms. You can sponsor an advert in which you're in a position to so that more people can view it. As is the case with interesting ideas, it goes viral. Scores of people will view your pictures, watch your videos or read the articles. Even better, they share the content and just like that; it's exposed to a larger audience. Fortunately, social media platforms keep track of it all. Numbers sure don't lie. Use those hits, likes, shares, follows and comments in your next pitch. People are drawn to ideas that have fascinated other people. They don't want to be left behind, they want to be part of the excitement too.

Even with the most savage persuasion skills, you won't always get a positive reply. And that is ok. Perhaps the ideas you're presenting are not fit for that particular time. Or for that particular audience. Don't take it personally. Don't cut links or begrudge people who don't accept your ideas. You can still relate to other matters. A rejection of your ideas or views should not be viewed as the rejecting of you as a person. Maintain mutual relationships. It's a small world, you never know when your paths will cross.

Chapter 21: Master Public Speaking Skills

'Is public speaking a preserve for some and not others?' We constantly ask ourselves every time we watch public figures giving their speeches (or any other presentations) so effortlessly. For most of us, even the mere thought of speaking before an audience is nerve-wracking.

While some are better than others, public speaking can be done by anyone with adequate preparation. The success of the talk is determined way before it is presented - the preparation stage. It is comforting to know that even those who seem so natural at it, like politicians, go through weeks if not months of getting ready.

In her new autobiography Becoming, former first lady Michelle Obama speaks of the rigorous preparations that would take place before making any presentation. The president was better at it, but watching her speeches too, you have to admit that she too put her best foot forward. Here's how a typical preparation stage should look like:

Gather the content: Depending on your audience, come up with the content that best appeals to them. This could be from the library, internet and other forms of archives. Write your speech in the order of introduction, main points than the summary. Writing a speech should not be so casual. Let your personality be felt. If you just put together information from research, there will be nothing unique in that. Anyone can access such information. Add a bit of your personal story regarding your upbringing, education, marriage, career, world views and so on. Blend those experiences into your topic and use them to add depth to your points.

Practice: It is one thing to speak in your mind, and quite another to speak aloud. Aren't we all so eloquent in our minds? How many times have you prepared the things you will say for instance in a meeting, only to get tongue-tied when your turn to speak comes? Start by reading the presentation out loud. Eliminate any difficult words that are difficult to pronounce. Start by reading with an even tone, just to internalize the content. Then try reading with the proper tonal variation. Adjust your tone when making strong assertions. Alternate between a hard and a soft voice depending on the content.

Practice in front of an audience of your family and buddies. An imaginary audience denies you the sensation of speaking to people. There are sensations that you go through when people are looking at you with those expectant eyes, waiting to hear what you have to say. That instance can easily leave you in jitters, ruining your opening moment. Speaking to people helps you get ready for the emotions.

What about practicing in front of the mirror? While it is a common option, it is rather distracting. The aim is to see how you appear as you speak, but other things too are likely to catch your attention. Like the rashes building up on your chin. Or the blackheads that can't seem to go away. Or that thinning hairline that has rejected all your remedies. Your attention is drawn to how you look, instead of how you speak. The audience is not going to be bothered by those details, so you better focus on what actually counts.

Get familiar: Getting onto the stage brings a lot of anxiety. Even experienced speakers will tell you that those first few moments after getting on stage are nerve-wracking. If you can visit the venue beforehand. Pictures and videos will do if you're far away. Study them until the venue feels familiar to you, like a place that you visit often. Have a look at the stage. How big is it? Which side does it face? Which side will you enter from? Will the microphone be fixed or portable? Which form of visual aid will work best? You may have planned a dramatic speech with lots of movement, only to find the microphone is fixed and you have to stand on the lectern the whole time. Acquainting yourself with the stage helps boost your confidence.

Comfortable Attire: What do your clothes have to do with your presentation? A lot. If any bit of your attire is uncomfortable, it will distract you from your core mandate of delivering a message. This especially goes for ladies. Is your skirt/dress too short when you sit? Remember you might be sitting at the front facing the audience. You don't want to keep pulling it down. Adjusting your clothes constantly reflects poorly on your confidence. Cover up appropriately in decent formal wear. Nothing too catchy, as the attention of the audience might be distracted. The men will do with a well-fitting suit.

When the day of the speech comes, arrive early. All the preparation above can be thrown into jeopardy if you get there late. To begin with, you'll be anxious, and anxiety clouds your thoughts. Arriving late also reflects badly on the audience. Punctuality always makes a good first impression.

1. Catchy opening

You're finally on stage for the long-awaited presentation. How does that feel? Having prepared with the tips above, chances are you're confident and rearing to go. The audience is waiting with bated breath. Your opening statement is like that first bite of a meal, it forms a permanent perception. Start with something personal. Or a joke. In a different chapter where we discussed the use of humor in conversation, we agreed that opinion is divided regarding the use of jokes to start presentations. What is the worst that can happen? The joke can flop, and you'll have started on a low note.

However, you do not have to wait to coin or test the joke there. You can prepare it in advance. That's right, jokes are often prepared in advance, even those made to sound like they've just been composed in the spur of the moment. If you can open with a funny joke, you're off to a good start. A personal story also grabs the attention of the listeners and gives them a personal attachment to you. Set a high momentum right from the start and the audience will be hanging on to your every word.

2. Body language

What you portray with your body is just as important as what you say. Move around the stage as space allows. This shows you're relaxed and confident. Stand with your feet slightly apart. Use appropriate gestures. Make random eye contacts. Not too long though; you don't want to make anyone uncomfortable. Your eyes should be trained right above their heads. When you look at the audience at that angle, it looks like eye contact from down there. Speak slowly. We're referring to the pace here, not the volume. Rushing over your content makes you sound nervous. Project your voice with clarity. Let the volume of the microphone be adjusted if you feel like you have to shout. Vary your tone appropriately throughout the speech. Let your body language be in tandem with your words.

3. Show confidence

It is one thing to be confident, and quite another to show it. Can the listeners tell that you're confident? That will inform their expectations. There are those speakers that make a poor first impression and are dismissed from the start. You can see it in the demeanor of the listeners. They sink back into their chairs and look bored. Such a speaker will have a hard time salvaging the situation.

How people perceive you affect how you behave. If the listeners sit up and look eager when you begin to speak, you'll feel energized to do just that. Once you portray confidence from the onset, you raise the expectation, and that perception bounces right back to you.

Enjoy yourself as well. Be excited about the opportunity to speak and the topic at hand. Speak with enthusiasm. Smile. Once you radiate these traits, the crowd will follow suit to the end. Make sure that you have some actionable points at the end, something the listeners can go try out on their own.

Along with knowing what to do, is knowing what not to do. One of the most common mistakes of speakers is talking down on the audience. Speakers are generally considered to be experts, right? Let's say you're an expert in lifestyle diseases. You want to tell your audience that their lifestyle and diet choices increase their risk of disease. You have to say it reasonably, without criticizing them. Don't say something like, 'when is the last time you had a fresh home-cooked salad? You can't expect to live on junk!' To you, it might sound like a motivation to initiate change, but it sounds plain offensive. Such mass condemnation is a no-no.

Avoid too many numbers, which is referred to as data-centric content. Some speakers are of the opinion that numbers equal intelligence. They present statistics after another, each with a larger number than the last. Unfortunately, such a strategy does not work. The listeners will quickly lose interest.

It is the simple human story that people connect to. Not figures. Tell them how your topic affects their lives. Give them snippets of your own life, discuss common human challenges. Suggest solutions that people can work on together. You may point out the negatives, but don't dwell on them. Nobody wants a presentation that sounds like one long rant. Give people hope. That is what the human heart yearns for. Optimism is in short supply around us. Be a generous supplier. Once you set yourself apart as a speaker who leaves people feeling better than he found them, you can be sure they will want to listen to you time and again.

Chapter 22: 7-Day Challenge

Day 1: Starting a conversation

- Write down the techniques of starting a conversation
- Pick one that you find easiest to use
- Formulate 5 scenarios in your mind where you can use them
- Pick up a conversation with a colleague that you've never spoken to

Day 2: Effective listening

- Maintain eye contact when someone is speaking to you
- Listen to somebody attentively for 5 minutes
- Write down what you understood from the conversation and let them confirm it
- Have someone listen to you attentively for 5 minutes and feel the difference

Day 3: Body language

- Smile at strangers and watch their reaction

- Firmly shake the hands of your senior, possibly one you've not interacted with before
- Strike the power pose and feel the difference

Day 4: Handling conflict

- Think of past scenarios of conflict and attempt to solve them in your mind
- Practice diplomatic dialogue
- Resolve a conflict amongst your friends

Day 5: Dealing with shyness and social anxiety

- Start a conversation with a stranger
- Go to an event that you do not know anyone
- Speak out your mind in a meeting

Day 6: Public speaking

- Tape yourself speaking for 5 minutes
- Evaluate and determine what to correct
- Give a 10-minute speech to an imaginary audience in your house

Day 7: Hone persuasion skills

- Sell an item to a stranger

- Revisit an idea that had been rejected and present it again

Conclusion

Congratulations on making it to the end of this book on communication skills. We set out to offer you comprehensive training on a diverse range of aspects of communication. The aim here was to ensure that you develop your social skills, improve empathy, learn how to be persuasive and achieve successful relationships in all areas of your life. It is our hope that this information will get you started on a journey to acquire and improve these skills.

If you've lived with poor social skills for the better part of your life, you know how distressing that can be. You cringe at the mere idea of being in a social function. You can hardly start a conversation, so you hang out at the corner waiting for the first chance to make your exit. At work, you can't bring yourself to make presentations. The idea of speaking in public is unfathomable. Your relationships suffer in the process, as communication is the bedrock of associations.

Fortunately, your story does not have to end like that. With all the tips and guidelines that you've just read through, you can tell that your situation is about to change, right? These skills take practice. There are those who are naturals at it, but most good speakers have taken years to hone their skills. Now it is your turn.

You must have come across the 7-day challenge that seeks to teach you to among other things start a conversation, listen attentively, portray the correct body language, deal with difficult people, speak in public among others.

Try out the challenge several times. You may not see an obvious change in the first couple of weeks, but that does not mean that there's no progress taking place. For instance, you may still feel shy and anxious every time that you have to walk into a room full of people. Do not give up. Keep trying. Keep practicing the activities listed in the challenge. Before you know it, you'll be comfortable doing some of the things that you could not have attempted before.

You can also formulate your own plan to complement the challenge. Put yourself out there. Do the things, and go to places that you have always avoided. Get a partner who has good communication skills to work with you. He/she will hold you accountable, help monitor your progress and point out your strengths and weaknesses so you can know where to improve.

This is not the kind of book that you read once and keep away. This one you keep close and refer from time to time. For instance, if you're dealing with a skeptic, or a difficult person, or a conflict, you can always come back and check how to go about it. You can also direct your colleagues to acquire the book so that you can all improve your communication skills so that your workplace will be more cohesive.

Feel free to drop us a review as well, so that others can find this book and benefit just like you have.